Viking Tales of Old Iceland 1

Original Texts, Translations, and Word Lists

Translated by
Matthew Leigh Embleton

Viking Tales of Old Iceland 1

The Tale of the Story-Wise Icelander (*Old Norse*) 3
The Tale of the Story-Wise Icelander (*Old Icelandic*) 14
The Tale of Ívarr Son of Ingimundr (*Old Norse*) 26
The Tale of Ívarr Son of Ingimundr (*Old Icelandic*) 43
The Tale of Thorstein Shiver (*Old Norse*) 61
The Tale of Thorstein Shiver (*Old Icelandic*) 81
The Tale of Thiðrandi and Thórhall (*Old Norse*) 103
The Tale of Thiðrandi and Thórhall (*Old Icelandic*) 127

Cover: Old Norse text over an outline of Iceland. Author's design.

The original Old Norse and Old Icelandic texts are in the public domain.
These translations ©2022 Matthew Leigh Embleton
©2025 Matthew Leigh Embleton (This Edition)

Acknowledgments

I have long been fascinated by languages and history, and I am very grateful to the special people in my life who have supported and encouraged me in my work. Thank you for believing in me. You know who you are.

Introduction

Old Norse is a North Germanic language spoken by inhabitants of Scandinavia from about the 7th to the 15th centuries. Old Icelandic is a variety of Old West Norse that emerged during the Norse settlement of Iceland in the second half of the 9th century. The rich tradition of Icelandic story telling survived by oral tradition over several centuries before being written down in the 13th Century. The Tales of Icelanders are known as Íslendingaþættir. The word 'þáttr' (plural: 'þættir') translates as a strand of rope or a yarn, comparable to the word 'yarn' in English sometimes used to refer to a story.

The texts are presented in Old Norse and Old Icelandic, in their original form, with a literal word-for-word line-by-line translation, and a Modern English translation, all side-by-side. In this way, it is possible to see and feel how the worked and how it has evolved. This book is designed to be of use and interest to anyone with a passion for the Old Norse or Old Icelandic language, Norse history, or languages and history in general.

The Tale of the Story-Wise Icelander (Old Norse)

The Tale of the Story-Wise Icelander (*Old Norse*)

Old Norse	Literal	English
Svá barst at eitthvert sumar, at einn íslenzkr maðr, ungr ok fráligr, kom til [Haralds] konungs ok bað hann ásjá.	So bore to one summer, that one Icelander man, young and bright, came to [Harald's] the-king and bid him assistance.	So it happened one summer that an Icelander man, young and bright, came to the king and asked for his assistance.
Konungr spurði, ef hann kynni nökkura fræði, en hann lézt kunna sögur.	The-king asked, if he knew-of any wisdom, that he let could say.	The king asked if he knew of any lore that he could tell stories.
Þá sagði konungr, at hann mun [taka] við honum, en hann skal þess skyldr at skemmta ávallt, er vildi, hverrgi sem hann bæði.	Then said the-king, that he would [take] with him, but he shall this should to entertain always, as willed, each who he bid.	Then the king said that he would keep him but he should always entertain anyone who asked him.
Ok svá gerir hann, ok er hann vinsæll við hirðina, ok gefa þeir honum klæði, ok konungr gefr honum vápn í hönd sér,	And so did he, and was he popular with king's-men, and gave they to-him clothes, and the-king gave him weapons in hand for-him,	And so he did, and he was popular with the king's men, and they gave him clothes and the king gave him weapons in his hand.
ok líðr nú svá fram til jóla.	and Passed now so from until Yule.	And so it passed until yule.
Þá ógleðr Íslending, ok spyrr konungr, hví þat gegndi.	Then un-glad Icelander, and asked the-king, what the reason.	Then the Icelander grew sad and the king asked what the reason was.
Hann kvað mislyndi sína til koma.	He said mood his towards came.	He said that this was a bad mood that had come on.
Ekki mun þat vera, segir konungr, "ok mun ek geta til.	Not could that be, said the-king, "and could I guess to.	"That could not be", said the king, "and I shall guess what it is.
Þess get ek til", segir hann, "at nú muni uppi sögur þínar.	This guess I to", said he, "that now recalled up stories yours.	This is my guess", he said, "that all the stories you remember you have now told.
Þú hefir ávallt skemmt í vetr, hverjum sem beiðzt hefir.	You have always entertained about winter, everyone who bid has.	You have always entertained this winter everyone who has asked you.
Mun þér nú illt þykkja, at þrjóti at jólunum".	Could you now ill valued, as-a failure this Yule".	Shall you now feel bad about yule".

The Tale of the Story-Wise Icelander (Old Norse)

Old Norse	Literal	English
Jafnt er svá sem þú getr, segir hann. "Ein er sagan eftir, ok þori ek þá eigi hér at segja, því at þat er útferðarsaga þín".	Equal is so as you guess, said he. "One of the-saga remaining, and dare I this not here to say, because that this is out-faring-saga yours".	"It is equal to your guess", he said, "one of the sagas is remaining and I dare not tell this here, because this is the saga of your travels".
Konungr mælti:	The-king spoke:	The king said:
Sú er ok svá sagan, at mér er mest um at heyra, ok skaltu nú ekki skemmta til jólanna fram, er menn eru nú í starfi,	So is also such saga, that to-me is most about to hear, and shall-you now none entertain until Yule forwards, as the-men are now to work,	"So it is the saga that I most want to hear, and you shall now not entertain anyone until yule, as the men are now busy with work.
en jóladag skaltu til taka þessar sögu ok segja af nökkurn spöl, ok ek mun svá til stilla með þér, at jafndrjúg mun verða sagan ok jólin.	but Yule-day shall-you to take this saga and say of something short, and I shall so to still with to-you, that equal-long shall be said also Yule.	But on the day of yule, take to this saga and tell a short amount of it, and I shall arrange it with you that the saga will be as long as yule.
Nú eru drykkjur miklar of jólin, ok má skömmum við sitja at hlýða skemmtan, ok ekki muntu á finna, meðan þú segir, hvárt mér þykkir vel eða illa.	Now they-are drinking much about Yule, and may-be short with sitting and listening-to entertainment, and not shall to find, while you say, whether I think well or ill.	Now they are drinking a lot at yule and they may have little time to sit and listen to stories, and you shall not be able to see whether I think I am pleased or not".
Nú er þat ok, at Íslendingr segir söguna, hefr upp jóladag ok segir of hríð, ok biðr konungr brátt hætta.	Now was it and, the Icelander said the-saga, had upped Yule-day and said of awhile, and asked the-king soon concluded.	Now it was and the Icelander told the saga, he began on the day of yule and spoke a while but the king soon asked him to stop.
Taka menn at drekka, ok ræða margir um, at þó sé djörfung í þessu, er hann Íslendingr segir þessa sögu, eða hversu konungi muni virðast.	Took men to drinking, and discussed many about, that though his boldness in this, that he The-Icelander said this saga, or how-so the-king would worth.	The men took to drinking and many discussed how bold it was of the Icelander to tell this saga, or how the king would value it.
Sumum þykkir hann vel segja, en sumir vinnast minna at.	Some thought he well said, but some won less of.	Some of them thought the saga went well but some valued it less.
Ferr svá fram of jólin.	Went so forwards about Yule.	And so it went during yule.
Konungr var vandr at, at hlýtt væri vel, ok stenzt þat á með umstilli konungs, er lokit er sögunni ok jólin þrýtr.	The-king was particularly that, to listen should-be well, and stood it about with about-guidance the-king's, was ended the saga and Yule ended.	The king was particular that it should be listened to well and with the king's guidance the saga ended and yule ended together.

The Tale of the Story-Wise Icelander (Old Norse)

Old Norse	Literal	English
Ok it þrettánda kveld, er lokit var sögunni áðr of daginn, mælti konungr:	And the thirteenth evening, when ended was the-saga earlier of the-day, spoke the-king:	At the thirteenth evening after the saga was told, the king spoke:
Er þér eigi forvitni á, Íslendingr, segir hann, "hversu mér líkar sagan?"	Are you not for-knowing about, Icelander, said he, "how-so to-me liked the-saga?"	"Are you curious, Icelander", he said, "how I liked the saga?"
Hræddr em ek um, herra, segir hann.	Scared am I about, lord, said he.	"I am scared to know, my lord", he said.
Konungr mælti:	The-king spoke:	The king spoke:
Mér þykkir allvel, ok hvergi verr en efni eru til, eða hverr kenndi þér söguna?	I thought all-well, and neither worse than the-matter was to, but who taught you the-saga?	"I thought it was all good and no worse than the matter was, but who taught you the saga?"
Hann svarar:	He answered:	He answered:
Þat var vanði minn út á landinu, at ek fór hvert sumar til þings, ok namk hvert sumar af sögunni nökkut at Halldóri Snorrasyni.	It was custom mine out-in the country, that I travelled each summer to assembly, and took each summer of saga something from Halldor Snorrason.	"It was my habit out in my country that I travelled each summer to the assembly, and I learned each summer something of the saga from Halldor Snorrason".
Þá er eigi kynligt, segir konungr, "at þú kunnir vel, ok mun þér at gæfu verða, ok ver með mér velkominn, ok skal þat heimilt ávallt, er þú vill".	Then is not extraordinary, said the-king, "that you know well, and shall to-you of gifted be, and be with me welcome, and shall it allow all-full, as you wish".	"Then it is no wonder", said the king, "that you know it well, and you shall be gifted and welcome with me and I shall grant you as you wish".
Konungr fekk honum góðan kaupeyri, ok varð hann þroskamaðr.	The-king gave him good wares, and was he vigorous-man.	The king gave him good wares and he was a vigorous man.

Word List (Old Norse to English)

Word List (Old Norse to English)

Old Norse	English

A, a

af	of
allvel	all-well
at	and, as-a, from, of, that, the, this, to

Á, á

á	about, the, to
áðr	earlier
ásjá	assistance
ávallt	all-full, always

B, b

bað	bid
bæði	bid
barst	bore
beiðzt	bid
biðr	asked
brátt	soon

D, d

daginn	the-day
djörfung	boldness
drekka	drinking
drykkjur	drinking

E, e

eða	but, or
ef	if
efni	the-matter
eftir	remaining
eigi	not
Ein	one
einn	one
eitthvert	one

Old Norse	English
ek	I
ekki	none, not
em	am
en	but, than, that
Er	are, as, is, of, that, the, was, when
eru	are, they-are, was

F, f

fekk	gave
Ferr	went
finna	find
fór	travelled
forvitni	for-knowing
fræði	wisdom
fráligr	bright
fram	forwards, from

G, g

gæfu	gifted
gefa	gave
gefr	gave
gegndi	reason
gerir	did
get	guess
geta	guess
getr	guess
góðan	good

H, h

hætta	concluded
Halldóri	Halldor (name)
hann	he, him
Haralds	Harald's (name)
hefir	has, have
hefr	had
heimilt	allow
hér	here

Word List (Old Norse to English)

Old Norse	English
herra	lord
heyra	hear
hirðina	king's-men
hlýða	listening-to
hlýtt	listen
hönd	hand
honum	him, to-him
Hræddr	scared
hríð	awhile
hvárt	whether
hvergi	neither
hverjum	everyone
hverr	who
hverrgi	each
hversu	how-so
hvert	each
hví	what

I, i

líðr	passed
illa	ill
illt	ill
it	the

Í, í

í	about, in, to
Íslending	Icelander
Íslendingr	Icelander, the-Icelander
íslenzkr	Icelander

J, j

jafndrjúg	equal-long
Jafnt	equal
jóla	Yule
jóladag	Yule-day
jólanna	Yule
jólin	Yule
jólunum	Yule

K, k

kaupeyri	wares
kenndi	taught
klæði	clothes
kom	came
koma	came
konungi	the-king
Konungr	the-king
konungs	the-king, the-king's
kunna	could
kunnir	know
kvað	said
kveld	evening
kynligt	extraordinary
kynni	knew-of

L, l

landinu	country
lézt	let
líkar	liked
lokit	ended

M, m

má	may-be
maðr	man
mælti	spoke
margir	many
með	with
meðan	while
menn	men, the-men
mér	I, me, to-me
mest	most
miklar	much
minn	mine
minna	less
mislyndi	mood
mun	could, shall, would
muni	recalled, would
muntu	shall

Word List (Old Norse to English)

Old Norse	English
N, n	
namk	took
nökkura	any
nökkurn	something
nökkut	something
nú	now
O, o	
of	about, of
ok	also, and
Ó, ó	
ógleðr	un-glad
R, r	
ræða	discussed
S, s	
sagan	saga, said, the-saga
sagði	said
sé	his
segir	said, say
segja	said, say
sem	as, who
sér	for-him
sína	his
sitja	sitting
skal	shall
skaltu	shall-you
skemmt	entertained
skemmta	entertain
skemmtan	entertainment
skömmum	short
skyldr	should
Snorrasyni	Snorrason (name)
sögu	saga
söguna	the-saga
sögunni	saga, the-saga
sögur	say, stories
spöl	short
spurði	asked
spyrr	asked
starfi	work
stenzt	stood
stilla	still
Sú	so
sumar	summer
sumir	some
Sumum	some
svá	so, such
svarar	answered
T, t	
taka	take, took
til	to, towards, until
Þ, þ	
Þá	then, this
þat	it, that, the, this
þeir	they
þér	to-you, you
þess	this
þessa	this
þessar	this
þessu	this
þín	yours
þínar	yours
þings	assembly
þó	though
þori	dare
þrettánda	thirteenth
þrjóti	failure
þroskamaðr	vigorous-man
þrýtr	ended
Þú	you
því	because
þykkir	think, thought
þykkja	valued

8

Word List (Old Norse to English)

Old Norse   English

U, u

um	about
umstilli	about-guidance
ungr	young
upp	upped
uppi	up

Ú, ú

út	out-in
útferðarsaga	out-faring-saga

V, v

væri	should-be
vanði	custom
vandr	particularly
vápn	weapons
var	was
varð	was
vel	well
velkominn	welcome
ver	be
vera	be
verða	be
verr	worse
vetr	winter
við	with
vildi	willed
vill	wish
vinnast	won
vinsæll	popular
virðast	worth

Word List (English to Old Norse)

Word List (English to Old Norse)

English	Old Norse
A, a	
about	á, í, of, um
about-guidance	umstilli
all-full	ávallt
allow	heimilt
all-well	allvel
also	ok
always	ávallt
am	em
and	at, ok
answered	svarar
any	nökkura
are	Er, eru
as	er, sem
as-a	at
asked	biðr, spurði, spyrr
assembly	þings
assistance	ásjá
awhile	hríð
B, b	
be	ver, vera, verða
because	því
bid	bað, bæði, beiðzt
boldness	djörfung
bore	barst
bright	fráligr
but	eða, en
C, c	
came	kom, koma
clothes	klæði
concluded	hætta
could	kunna, mun
country	landinu
custom	vanði
D, d	
dare	þori
did	gerir
discussed	ræða
drinking	drekka, drykkjur
E, e	
each	hverrgi, hvert
earlier	áðr
ended	lokit, þrýtr
entertain	skemmta
entertained	skemmt
entertainment	skemmtan
equal	Jafnt
equal-long	jafndrjúg
evening	kveld
everyone	hverjum
extraordinary	kynligt
F, f	
failure	þrjóti
find	finna
for-him	sér
for-knowing	forvitni
forwards	fram
from	at, fram
G, g	
gave	fekk, gefa, gefr
gifted	gæfu
good	góðan
guess	get, geta, getr
H, h	

Word List (English to Old Norse)

English	*Old Norse*
had	*hefr*
Halldor (name)	*Halldóri*
hand	*hönd*
Harald's (name)	*Haralds*
has	*hefir*
have	*hefir*
he	*hann*
hear	*heyra*
here	*hér*
him	*hann, honum*
his	*sé, sína*
how-so	*hversu*

I, i

English	*Old Norse*
I	*ek, mér*
Icelander	*Íslending, Íslendingr, íslenzkr*
if	*ef*
ill	*illa, illt*
in	*í*
is	*er*
it	*þat*

K, k

knew-of	*kynni*
king's-men	*hirðina*
know	*kunnir*

L, l

less	*minna*
let	*lézt*
liked	*líkar*
listen	*hlýtt*
listening-to	*hlýða*
lord	*herra*

M, m

English	*Old Norse*
man	*maðr*
many	*margir*
may-be	*má*
me	*mér*
men	*menn*
mine	*minn*
mood	*mislyndi*
most	*mest*
much	*miklar*

N, n

neither	*hvergi*
none	*ekki*
not	*eigi, Ekki*
now	*nú*

O, o

of	*af, at, er, of*
one	*Ein, einn, eitthvert*
or	*eða*
out-faring-saga	*útferðarsaga*
out-in	*út*

P, p

particularly	*vandr*
passed	*líðr*
popular	*vinsæll*

R, r

reason	*gegndi*
recalled	*muni*
remaining	*eftir*

S, s

saga	*sagan, sögu, sögunni*

Word List (English to Old Norse)

English	Old Norse	English	Old Norse
said	kvað, sagan, sagði, segir, segja	though	þó
		thought	þykkir
say	segir, segja, sögur	to	á, at, í, til
scared	Hræddr	to-him	honum
shall	mun, muntu, skal	to-me	mér
shall-you	skaltu	took	namk, Taka
short	skömmum, spöl	towards	til
should	skyldr	to-you	þér
should-be	væri	travelled	fór
sitting	sitja		
Snorrason (name)	Snorrasyni		

U, u

English	Old Norse
so	Sú, svá
some	sumir, Sumum
something	nökkurn, nökkut
soon	brátt
spoke	mælti
still	stilla
stood	stenzt
stories	sögur
such	svá
summer	sumar

un-glad	ógleðr
until	til
up	uppi
upped	upp

T, t

V, v

valued	þykkja
vigorous-man	þroskamaðr

take	taka
taught	kenndi
than	en
that	at, en, er, þat
the	á, at, er, it, þat
the-day	daginn
the-Icelander	Íslendingr
the-king	konungi, Konungr, konungs
the-king's	konungs
the-matter	efni
the-men	menn
then	Þá
the-saga	sagan, söguna, sögunni
they	þeir
they-are	eru
think	þykkir
thirteenth	þrettánda
this	at, þá, þat, þess, þessa, þessar, þessu

W, w

wares	kaupeyri
was	er, eru, var, varð
weapons	vápn
welcome	velkominn
well	vel
went	Ferr
what	hví
when	er
whether	hvárt
while	meðan
who	hverr, sem
willed	vildi
winter	vetr
wisdom	fræði
wish	vill
with	með, við
won	vinnast
work	starfi
worse	verr

Word List (English to Old Norse)

English	Old Norse

worth | *virðast*
would | *mun, muni*

Y, y

you | *þér, Þú*
young | *ungr*
yours | *þín, þínar*
Yule | *jóla, jólanna, jólin, jólunum*
Yule-day | *jóladag*

The Tale of the Story-Wise Icelander (*Old Icelandic*)

Old Icelandic	Literal	English
Svo barst að eitthvert sumar að einn íslenskur maður, ungur og frálegur, kom til konungs og bað hann ásjá.	So bore to one summer that one Icelander man, young and bright, came to the-king and bid him assistance.	So it happened one summer that an Icelander man, young and bright, came to the king and asked for his assistance.
Konungur spurði ef hann kynni nokkverja fræði en hann lést kunna sögur.	The-king asked if he knew-of any wisdom that he let could say.	The king asked if he knew of any lore that he could tell stories.
Þá sagði konungur að hann mun taka við honum en hann skal þess skyldur að skemmta ávallt er vildi, hvergi sem hann bæði.	Then said the-king that he would take with him but he shall this should to entertain always as willed, each who he bid-(asked).	Then the king said that he would keep him but he should always entertain anyone who asked him.
Og svo gerir hann og er hann vinsæll við hirðina og gefa þeir honum klæði og konungur gefur honum vopn í hönd sér.	And so did he and was he popular with king's-men and gave they to-him clothes and the-king gave him weapons in hand for-him.	And so he did, and he was popular with the king's men, and they gave him clothes and the king gave him weapons in his hand.
Og líður nú svo fram til jóla.	And passed now so from until yule.	And so it passed until yule.
Þá ógleður Íslending og spyr konungur hví það gegndi.	Then un-glad-(sad) Icelander and asked the-king what the reason.	Then the Icelander grew sad and the king asked what the reason was.
Hann kvað mislyndi sína til koma.	He said mood his towards came.	He said that this was a bad mood that had come on.
"Ekki mun það vera", segir konungur, "og mun eg geta til.	"Not could that be", said the-king, "and could I guess to.	"That could not be", said the king, "and I shall guess what it is.
Þess get eg til", segir hann, "að nú muni uppi sögur þínar.	This guess I to", said he, "that now recalled up stories yours.	This is my guess", he said, "that all the stories you remember you have now told.
Þú hefir ávallt skemmt í vetur hverjum sem beiðst hefir.	You have always entertained about winter everyone who bid-(asked) has.	You have always entertained this winter everyone who has asked you.
Mun þér nú illt þykja að þrjóti að jólunum".	Could you now ill valued as-a failure this yule".	Shall you now feel bad about yule".

The Tale of the Story-Wise Icelander (Old Icelandic)

Old Icelandic	Literal	English
"Jafnt er svo sem þú getur", segir hann, "ein er sagan eftir og þori eg þá eigi hér að segja því að það er útferðarsaga þín".	"Equal is so as you guess", said he, "one of the-saga remaining and dare I this not here to say because that this is out-faring-saga yours".	"It is equal to your guess", he said, "one of the sagas is remaining and I dare not tell this here, because this is the saga of your travels".
Konungur mælti:	The-king spoke:	The king said:
"Sú er og svo sagan að mér er mest um að heyra og skaltu nú ekki skemmta til jólanna fram er menn eru nú í starfi.	"So is also such saga that to-me is most about to hear and shall-you now none entertain until yule forwards as the-men are now to work.	"So it is the saga that I most want to hear, and you shall now not entertain anyone until yule, as the men are now busy with work.
En jóladag skaltu til taka þessa sögu og segja af nokkvern spöl og eg mun svo til stilla með þér að jafndrjúg mun verða sagan og jólin.	But yule-day shall-you to take this saga and say of something short and I shall so to still with to-you that equal-long shall be said also yule.	But on the day of yule, take to this saga and tell a short amount of it, and I shall arrange it with you that the saga will be as long as yule.
Nú eru drykkjur miklar of jólin og má skömmum við sitja að hlýða skemmtan og ekki muntu á finna meðan þú segir hvort mér þykir vel eða illa".	Now they-are drinking much about yule and may-be short with sitting and listening-to entertainment and not shall to find while you say whether I think well or ill".	Now they are drinking a lot at yule and they may have little time to sit and listen to stories, and you shall not be able to see whether I think I am pleased or not".
Nú er það og að Íslendingur segir söguna, hefur upp jóladag og segir of hríð og biður konungur brátt hætta.	Now was it and the Icelander said the-saga, had upped yule-day and said of awhile and asked the-king soon concluded.	Now it was and the Icelander told the saga, he began on the day of yule and spoke a while but the king soon asked him to stop.
Taka menn að drekka og ræða margir um að þó sé djörfung í þessu er hann Íslendingur segir þessa sögu eða hversu konungi muni virðast.	Took men to drinking and discussed many about that though his boldness in this that he The-Icelander said this saga or how-so the-king would worth-(value).	The men took to drinking and many discussed how bold it was of the Icelander to tell this saga, or how the king would value it.
Sumum þykir hann vel segja en sumir vinnast minna að.	Some thought he well said but some won less of.	Some of them thought the saga went well but some valued it less.
Fer svo fram of jólin.	Went so forwards about yule.	And so it went during yule.

The Tale of the Story-Wise Icelander (Old Icelandic)

Old Icelandic	Literal	English
Konungur var vandur að að hlýtt væri vel og stenst það á með umstilli konungs er lokið er sögunni og jólin þrýtur.	The-king was particularly that to listen should-be well and stood it about with about-guidance the-king's was ended the saga and yule ended.	The king was particular that it should be listened to well and with the king's guidance the saga ended and yule ended together.
Og hið þrettánda kveld er lokið var sögunni áður of daginn mælti konungur:	And the thirteenth evening when ended was the-saga earlier of the-day spoke the-king:	At the thirteenth evening after the saga was told, the king spoke:
"Er þér eigi forvitni á Íslendingur", segir hann, "hversu mér líkar sagan?".	"Are you not for-knowing-(curious) about Icelander", said he, "how-so to-me liked the-saga?"	"Are you curious, Icelander", he said, "how I liked the saga?"
"Hræddur em eg um herra", segir hann.	"Scared am I about lord", said he.	"I am scared to know, my lord", he said.
Konungur mælti:	The-king spoke:	The king spoke:
"Mér þykir allvel og hvergi verr en efni eru til eða hver kenndi þér söguna?".	"I thought all-well and neither worse than the-matter was to but who taught you the-saga?"	"I thought it was all good and no worse than the matter was, but who taught you the saga?"
Hann svarar:	He answered:	He answered:
"Það var vandi minn út á landinu að eg fór hvert sumar til þings og nam eg hvert sumar af sögunni nakkvað að Halldóri Snorrasyni".	"It was custom mine out-in the country that I travelled each summer to assembly and took I each summer of saga something from Halldor Snorrason".	"It was my habit out in my country that I travelled each summer to the assembly, and I learned each summer something of the saga from Halldor Snorrason".
"Þá er eigi kynlegt", segir konungur, "að þú kunnir vel og mun þér að gæfu verða og ver með mér velkominn og skal það heimilt ávallt er þú vilt.	"Then is not extraordinary", said the-king, "that you know well and shall to-you of gifted be and be with me welcome and shall it allow all-full as you wish.	"Then it is no wonder", said the king, "that you know it well, and you shall be gifted and welcome with me and I shall grant you as you wish".
Konungur fékk honum góðan kaupeyri og varð hann þroskamaður.	The-king gave him good wares and was he vigorous-man.	The king gave him good wares and he was a vigorous man.

Word List (Old Icelandic to English)

Word List (Old Icelandic to English)

Old Icelandic	English

A, a

að	and, as-a, from, of, that, the, this, to
af	of
allvel	all-well

Á, á

á	about, the, to
áður	earlier
ásjá	assistance
ávallt	all-full, always

B, b

bað	bid
bæði	bid
barst	bore
beiðst	bid
biður	asked
brátt	soon

D, d

daginn	the-day
djörfung	boldness
drekka	drinking
drykkjur	drinking

E, e

eða	but, or
ef	if
efni	the-matter
eftir	remaining
eg	I
eigi	not
ein	one
einn	one

Old Icelandic	English
eitthvert	one
ekki	none, not
em	am
en	but, than, that
er	are, as, is, of, that, the, was, when
eru	are, they-are, was

F, f

fékk	gave
fer	went
finna	find
fór	travelled
forvitni	for-knowing
fræði	wisdom
frálegur	bright
fram	forwards, from

G, g

gæfu	gifted
gefa	gave
gefur	gave
gegndi	reason
gerir	did
get	guess
geta	guess
getur	guess
góðan	good

H, h

hætta	concluded
halldóri	Halldor (name)
hann	he, him
hefir	has, have
hefur	had
heimilt	allow
hér	here
herra	lord

Word List (Old Icelandic to English)

Old Icelandic	English
heyra	hear
hið	the
hirðina	king's-men
hlýða	listening-to
hlýtt	listen
hönd	hand
honum	him, to-him
hræddur	scared
hríð	awhile
hver	who
hvergi	each, neither
hverjum	everyone
hversu	how-so
hvert	each
hví	what
hvort	whether

I, i

illa	ill
illt	ill

Í, í

í	about, in, to
íslending	Icelander
íslendingur	Icelander, the-Icelander
íslenskur	Icelander

J, j

jafndrjúg	equal-long
jafnt	equal
jóla	yule
jóladag	yule-day
jólanna	yule
jólin	yule
jólunum	yule

K, k

Old Icelandic	English
kaupeyri	wares
kenndi	taught
klæði	clothes
kom	came
koma	came
konungi	the-king
konungs	the-king, the-king's
konungur	the-king
kunna	could
kunnir	know
kvað	said
kveld	evening
kynlegt	extraordinary
kynni	knew-of

L, l

landinu	country
lést	let
líður	passed
líkar	liked
lokið	ended

M, m

má	may-be
maður	man
mælti	spoke
margir	many
með	with
meðan	while
menn	men, the-men
mér	I, me, to-me
mest	most
miklar	much
minn	mine
minna	less
mislyndi	mood
mun	could, shall, would
muni	recalled, would
muntu	shall

N, n

18

Word List (Old Icelandic to English)

Old Icelandic	English
nakkvað	something
nam	took
nokkverja	any
nokkvern	something
nú	now

O, o

of	about, of
og	also, and

Ó, ó

ógleður	un-glad

R, r

ræða	discussed

S, s

sagan	saga, said, the-saga
sagði	said
sé	his
segir	said, say
segja	said, say
sem	as, who
sér	for-him
sína	his
sitja	sitting
skal	shall
skaltu	shall-you
skemmt	entertained
skemmta	entertain
skemmtan	entertainment
skömmum	short
skyldur	should
snorrasyni	Snorrason (name)
sögu	saga
söguna	the-saga
sögunni	saga, the-saga
sögur	say, stories
spöl	short
spurði	asked
spyr	asked
starfi	work
stenst	stood
stilla	still
sú	so
sumar	summer
sumir	some
sumum	some
svarar	answered
svo	so, such

T, t

taka	take, took
til	to, towards, until

Þ, þ

þá	then, this
það	it, that, the, this
þeir	they
þér	to-you, you
þess	this
þessa	this
þessar	this
þessu	this
þín	yours
þínar	yours
þings	assembly
þó	though
þori	dare
þrettánda	thirteenth
þrjóti	failure
þroskamaður	vigorous-man
þrýtur	ended
þú	you
því	because
þykir	think, thought
þykja	valued

Word List (Old Icelandic to English)

Old Icelandic   English

U, u

um	about
umstilli	about-guidance
ungur	young
upp	upped
uppi	up

Ú, ú

út	out-in
útferðarsaga	out-faring-saga

V, v

væri	should-be
vandi	custom
vandur	particularly
var	was
varð	was
vel	well
velkominn	welcome
ver	be
vera	be
verða	be
verr	worse
vetur	winter
við	with
vildi	willed
vilt	wish
vinnast	won
vinsæll	popular
virðast	worth
vopn	weapons

Word List (English to Old Icelandic)

Word List (English to Old Icelandic)

English	*Old Icelandic*

A, a

about	*á, í, of, um*
about-guidance	*umstilli*
all-full	*ávallt*
allow	*heimilt*
all-well	*allvel*
also	*og*
always	*ávallt*
am	*em*
and	*að, og*
answered	*svarar*
any	*nokkverja*
are	*er, eru*
as	*er, sem*
as-a	*að*
asked	*biður, spurði, spyr*
assembly	*þings*
assistance	*ásjá*
awhile	*hríð*

B, b

be	*ver, vera, verða*
because	*því*
bid	*bað, bæði, beiðst*
boldness	*djörfung*
bore	*barst*
bright	*frálegur*
but	*eða, en*

C, c

came	*kom, koma*
clothes	*klæði*
concluded	*hætta*
could	*kunna, mun*
country	*landinu*
custom	*vandi*

D, d

dare	*þori*
did	*gerir*
discussed	*ræða*
drinking	*drekka, drykkjur*

E, e

each	*hvergi, hvert*
earlier	*áður*
ended	*lokið, þrýtur*
entertain	*skemmta*
entertained	*skemmt*
entertainment	*skemmtan*
equal	*jafnt*
equal-long	*jafndrjúg*
evening	*kveld*
everyone	*hverjum*
extraordinary	*kynlegt*

F, f

failure	*þrjóti*
find	*finna*
for-him	*sér*
for-knowing	*forvitni*
forwards	*fram*
from	*að, fram*

G, g

gave	*fékk, gefa, gefur*
gifted	*gæfu*
good	*góðan*
guess	*get, geta, getur*

H, h

Word List (English to Old Icelandic)

English	*Old Icelandic*	English	*Old Icelandic*
had	*hefur*	man	*maður*
Halldor (name)	*halldóri*	many	*margir*
hand	*hönd*	may-be	*má*
has	*hefir*	me	*mér*
have	*hefir*	men	*menn*
he	*hann*	mine	*minn*
hear	*heyra*	mood	*mislyndi*
here	*hér*	most	*mest*
him	*hann, honum*	much	*miklar*
his	*sé, sína*		
how-so	*hversu*		

N, n

neither	*hvergi*
none	*ekki*
not	*eigi, ekki*
now	*nú*

I, i

I	*eg, mér*
Icelander	*íslending, íslendingur, íslenskur*
if	*ef*
ill	*illa, illt*
in	*í*
is	*er*
it	*það*

O, o

of	*að, af, er, of*
one	*ein, einn, eitthvert*
or	*eða*
out-faring-saga	*útferðarsaga*
out-in	*út*

K, k

king's-men	*hirðina*
knew-of	*kynni*
know	*kunnir*

P, p

particularly	*vandur*
passed	*líður*
popular	*vinsæll*

L, l

less	*minna*
let	*lést*
liked	*líkar*
listen	*hlýtt*
listening-to	*hlýða*
lord	*herra*

R, r

reason	*gegndi*
recalled	*muni*
remaining	*eftir*

S, s

saga	*sagan, sögu, sögunni*

M, m

Word List (English to Old Icelandic)

English	*Old Icelandic*
said	*kvað, sagan, sagði, segir, segja*
say	*segir, segja, sögur*
scared	*hræddur*
shall	*mun, muntu, skal*
shall-you	*skaltu*
short	*skömmum, spöl*
should	*skyldur*
should-be	*væri*
sitting	*sitja*
Snorrason (name)	*snorrasyni*
so	*sú, svo*
some	*sumir, sumum*
something	*nakkvað, nokkvern*
soon	*brátt*
spoke	*mælti*
still	*stilla*
stood	*stenst*
stories	*sögur*
such	*svo*
summer	*sumar*

T, t

take	*taka*
taught	*kenndi*
than	*en*
that	*að, en, er, það*
the	*á, að, er, hið, það*
the-day	*daginn*
the-Icelander	*íslendingur*
the-king	*konungi, konungs, konungur*
the-king's	*konungs*
the-matter	*efni*
the-men	*menn*
then	*þá*
the-saga	*sagan, söguna, sögunni*
they	*þeir*
they-are	*eru*
think	*þykir*
thirteenth	*þrettánda*
this	*að, þá, það, þess, þessa, þessar, þessu*
though	*þó*
thought	*þykir*
to	*á, að, í, til*
to-him	*honum*
to-me	*mér*
took	*nam, taka*
towards	*til*
to-you	*þér*
travelled	*fór*

U, u

un-glad	*ógleður*
until	*til*
up	*uppi*
upped	*upp*

V, v

valued	*þykja*
vigorous-man	*þroskamaður*

W, w

wares	*kaupeyri*
was	*er, eru, var, varð*
weapons	*vopn*
welcome	*velkominn*
well	*vel*
went	*fer*
what	*hví*
when	*er*
whether	*hvort*
while	*meðan*
who	*hver, sem*
willed	*vildi*
winter	*vetur*
wisdom	*fræði*
wish	*vilt*
with	*með, við*
won	*vinnast*
work	*starfi*
worse	*verr*

Word List (English to Old Icelandic)

English	*Old Icelandic*
worth	*virðast*
would	*mun, muni*

Y, y

you	*þér, þú*
young	*ungur*
yours	*þín, þínar*
yule	*jóla, jólanna, jólin, jólunum*
yule-day	*jóladag*

A Word Comparison of Old Norse and Old Icelandic Words

A Word Comparison of Old Norse and Old Icelandic Words

Old Norse	Old Icelandic	English	Old Norse	Old Icelandic	English
áðr	áður	earlier	stenzt	stenst	stood
at	að	and	svá	svo	so
at	að	as-a	svá	svo	such
at	að	from	þat	það	it
at	að	of	þat	það	that
at	að	that	þat	það	the
at	að	the	þat	það	this
at	að	this	þroskamaðr	þroskamaður	vigorous-man
at	að	to	þrýtr	þrýtur	ended
beiðzt	beiðst	bid	þykkir	þykir	think
biðr	biður	asked	þykkir	þykir	thought
ek	eg	I	þykkja	þykja	valued
fekk	fékk	gave	ungr	ungur	young
Ferr	fer	went	vanði	vandi	custom
fráligr	frálegur	bright	vandr	vandur	particularly
gefr	gefur	gave	vápn	vopn	weapons
getr	getur	guess	vetr	vetur	winter
hefr	hefur	had	vill	vilt	wish
Hræddr	hræddur	scared			
hvárt	hvort	whether			
hverr	hver	who			
hverrgi	hvergi	each			
líðr	líður	passed			
Íslendingr	íslendingur	Icelander			
Íslendingr	íslendingur	the-Icelander			
íslenzkr	íslenskur	Icelander			
it	hið	the			
Konungr	konungur	the-king			
kynligt	kynlegt	extraordinary			
lézt	lést	let			
lokit	lokið	ended			
maðr	maður	man			
namk	nam	took			
nökkura	nokkverja	any			
nökkurn	nokkvern	something			
nökkut	nakkvað	something			
ógleðr	ógleður	un-glad			
ok	og	also			
ok	og	and			
skyldr	skyldur	should			
spyrr	spyr	asked			

The Tale of Ívarr Son of Ingimundr (*Old Norse*)

Old Norse	Literal	English
Í ÞEIMA hlut má marka, er nú mun ek segja, hverr dýrðarmaðr Eysteinn konungr var eða hve mjök hann var vinhollr ok hugkvæmr eftir at leita við sína ástmenn, hvat þeim væri at harmi.	In that part may-be marked, that now shall I say, who glorious-man Eystein king was and how much he was friend-whole and thoughtful after to seek with his beloved-friends, that theirs was of grief.	In part it may be said that I shall now say who the glorious king Eystein was and how much he was a good friend and thoughtful in seeking with his beloved friends what was their grief.
Sá maðr var með Eysteini konungi, er Ívarr hét ok var Ingimundarson, íslenzkr at ætt ok stórættaðr at kyni, vitr maðr ok skáld gott.	That man was with Eystein the-king, was Ivar named and was Son-of-Ingimundur, Icelander by ancestry and large-family to kin, wise man and poet good.	That man was with Eystein the king and was named Ivar and he was the son of Ingimundur, an Icelander by ancestry with a large family and kin, a wise man and a good poet.
Konungr virði hann mikils ok var til hans ástsamliga, sem sýnist í þessum hlut.	The-king worthed him much and was to him affectionate, as seems in this matter.	The king valued him very much and was affectionate to him as it seems in this matter.
Þorfinnr hét bróðir Ívars.	Thorfin was-named brother Ivar's.	Ivar's brother was named Thorfin.
Hann fór ok útan á fund Eysteins konungs ok naut þar mjök frá [mörgum mönnum] bróður síns.	He travelled and out to meet Eystein the-king and enjoyed there much from [many men] brother his.	He travelled out to meet Eystein the king and enjoyed much of his brother's popularity with many men there.
En honum þótti þat mikit, er hann skyldi eigi þykkja jafnmenni bróður síns ok þurfa hans at njóta, ok undi af því eigi með konungi ok bjóst út til Íslands.	But he thought it much, that he should not be-valued equal-to brother his and needed he to enjoy, and part off therefore not with the-king and prepare out to Iceland.	But he thought it was a bit much that he was not valued as equal to his brother, on whom he depended for that which he enjoyed, and therefore parted with the king and prepared to travel out to Iceland.
Ok áðr en þeir bræðr skilðist, mælti Ívarr, at Þorfiðr skyldi þau orð bera Oddnýju Jóansdóttur, at hon biði hans ok giftist eigi, lét sér um hana mest vera allra kvenna.	And before that they brothers parted, said Ivar, that Thorfin should then word carry Oddynja Joansdottir, that she wait-for him and be-married not, had he about her the-most being of-all women.	And before the brothers parted Ivar said that Thorfin should carry word to Oddynja Joansdottir for her to wait for him and not marry, for he held her above all other women.
Síðan ferr Þorfinnr út ok varð vel reiðfari ok tók þat ráð, at hann bað Oddnýjar sér til handa ok fekk hennar.	Then travelled Thorfin out and was well travelled and took the decision, that he ask Oddny her to hand and married her.	Then Thorfin fared out and travelled well, and he decided to ask Oddyn for her hand in marriage himself.

The Tale of Ívarr Son of Ingimundr (Old Norse)

Old Norse	Literal	English
Ok litlu síðar kom Ívarr út ok frá þetta ok þótti Þorfiðr illa hafa ór haft við sik, ok unir hann engu ok ferr aftr síðan til konungs ok er með honum í góðu yfirlæti sem fyrr.	And a-little later came Ivar out and of this and thought Thorfin bad having of had with him, and satisfied he-was none and travelled back afterwards to the-king and was with him in good favour as before.	And a little later Ivar came out to Iceland and heard about this, and thought that Thorfin had done bad to him, and he was most unsatisfied, and travelled back to the king and was held in good favour with him as before.
Ívarr tekr nú ógleði mikla, ok er konungr fann þat, heimtí hann Ívar til máls við sik ok spurði, hví hann væri svá ókátr, - "ok fyrr, er þér váruð með oss, var margs konar skemmtan at yðrum orðum,	Ivar took now sadness much, and as the-king found it, summoned he Ivar to speak with him and asked, why he was so displeased, "and before, when you were with us, were many kinds-of amusement from your words,	Ivar took to a great sadness and when the king noticed he summoned Ivar to speak with him and asked him why he was so displeased "Whereas before when you were with us, there was much amusement from your words.
ok eigi leita ek fyrir því eftir þessu, at eigi vita ek, at vér höfum ekki af gert við þik.	and not asking I for since after this, that not knew I, that we have not of done with you.	And I do not ask since we do know know if it is because we have wronged you.
Ertu ok svá vitr maðr, at eigi muntu grun draga af því, er eigi er, ok seg mér, hvat er".	You-are and such wise man, that not should-you suspicion drag of therefore, if not is, and say to-me, what is".	For you are such a wise man that you would not suspect a slight where none exists, and please tell me what it is".
Ívarr svaraði:	Ivar answered:	Ivar answered:
"Þat, sem er, herra, má ek ekki frá segja".	"That, which is, lord, may I not from say".	"What it is lord I may not say".
Konungr mælti:	The-King said:	The king said:
"Ek mun þá geta til.	"I should then guess to.	"Then I should gess it.
Eru nökkurir menn, þeir er þér getist eigi at?"	Is-there some man, they who to-you estimate not of?"	Is there some man who you do not hold in esteem?"
"Eigi er þat, herra", segir Ívarr.	"Not is that, lord", said Ivar.	"It is not that, lord", said Ivar.
Konungr mælti:	The-King said:	The king said:
"Þykkist þú af mér hafa minna sóma en þú vildir?"	"Seeming to-you of me have less honour that you wish?"	"Do you think of me that I have less honour than you wish?".
"Eigi er þat, herra", segir hann.	"Not is that, lord", said he.	"It is not that, lord", said he.

The Tale of Ívarr Son of Ingimundr (Old Norse)

Old Norse	Literal	English
"Hefir þú sét nökkura hluti", segir konungr, "þá er þér hafa svá mikit um fundizt hér í landinu?"	"Have you seen any things", said the-king, "then that to-you have so greatly about found here in the-land?"	"Have you seen anything", said the king, "that you have found in this land which you covet?".
Hann kveðr eigi þat vera.	He said not that was.	He said that it was not that.
"Vandast oss nú getan", segir konungr.	"Difficult ours now guessing", said the-king.	"It is now difficult for us to guess", said the king.
"Villtu hafa forræði nökkur yfir eignum nökkurum?"	"Will-you to-have power any over owning anything?"	"Do you wish to have authority over or some ownership of something?".
Hann neitti því.	He nothing such.	He said it was nothing as such.
"Eru nökkurar konur þær á yðru landi", segir konungr, "er þér sé eftirsjá at?"	"Are-there some woman therefore that your land", said the-king, "that you yourself look-back to?"	"Are there any women there in your land", said the king, "that you look back to with regret?".
Hann svaraði:	He answered:	He answered:
"Svá er, herra".	"So it-is, lord".	"So it is, lord".
Konungr mælti:	The-King said:	The king said:
"Ver eigi þar um hugsjúkr.	"Be not therefore about-it mind-sick.	"Therefore do not be anxious about it.
Þegar er várar, far þú út.	As-soon as spring, travel you out.	As soon as the spring comes you shall travel out.
Mun ek fá þér fé ok bréf mitt með innsigli til þeira manna, er ráða eigu, ok veit ek eigi þeira manna vánir, at eigi víkja eftir várum vinmælum eða ógnarorðum at gifta konuna".	Shall I give you wealth and letters mine with royal-seal to those men, who power posess, and know I not they people's hopes, that not give-in after our friendly-words or menacing-words to give-in-marriage this-woman".	I shall give you wealth and letters with a royal seal to those men who have the authority, and I do not know of anyone who will not give in after our friendly words or menacing words to give this woman in marriage".
Ívarr svaraði:	Ivar answered:	Ivar answered:
"Eigi má svá vera".	"Not may so be".	"It may not be so".
Konungr mælti:	The-King said:	The king said:

The Tale of Ívarr Son of Ingimundr (Old Norse)

Old Norse	Literal	English
"Engi veg má þess vera", segir konungr.	"No way may this be", said the-king.	"There is no way this may be", said the king.
"Því mun ek mæla framar, þó at annarr maðr eigi hana, þá mun ek þó ná, ef ek vil, þér til handa".	"Therefore shall I say from, yet that another man owns her, then shall I nevertheless get, if I wish, you to hand".	"Therefore I shall say that yet another man owns her, then I shall nevertheless get her if you wish for her hand".
Ívarr svaraði:	Ivar answered:	Ivar answered:
"Þungligar er farit málinu, herra.	"Is going the-matter lord, lord.	"This is where the matter becomes difficult, lord.
Bróðir minn á nú konuna".	Brother mine has now a-wife".	My brother now has her as a wife".
Þá mælti konungr:	Then said the-king:	Then the king said:
"Hverfum þar frá", segir hann.	"Let-us-go here from", said he.	"Then let us go from here", he said.
"Sé ek þá ráð til.	"Say I then advise to.	"I say then to advise.
Eftir jólin mun ek fara á veizlur, ok far þú með mér, ok muntu þar sjá margar kurteisar konur, ok ef eigi eru konungbornar, þá mun ek fá þér einhverja".	After Yule shall I travel to feasts, and travel you with me, and shall there see many polite women, and if none are kings-born, then shall I get you one".	After Yule I shall travel to feasts and you shall travel with me and you shall see there many polite women, and if there are no kings born, then I shall get you one".
Ívarr svaraði:	Ivar answered:	Ivar answered:
"Herra, því þungligar er komit mínu máli, at jafnan, er ek sé fagrar konur, þá minnir mik þessar konu, ok er æ því meiri minn harmr".	"Lord, because the-heavier has become my matter, to equally, that I see fair woman, then memory mine this woman, and is ever therefore greater my grief".	"Lord, because my matter has become heavier, equally when I see a fair woman then I have memory of this woman, and my grief is ever therefore greater".
Konungr mælti:	The-King said:	The king said:
"Þá mun ek gefa þér nökkur forræði ok eigur, sem ek bauð þér fyrr, ok skemmtir þú þér við þat".	"Then shall I give to-you some authority and ownership, which I offered you before, and amuse you yourself with that".	"Then I shall give to you some authority and ownership which I offered you before and you can amuse yourself with that".
Hann svaraði:	He answered:	He answered:

The Tale of Ívarr Son of Ingimundr (Old Norse)

Old Norse	Literal	English
"Ekki uni ek því".	"Not like I that".	"I do not like that".
Konungr mælti:	The-King said:	The king said:
"Þá fæ ek þér lausafé, ok ferr þú kaupferðir þangat til landa, sem þú vill".	"Then give I to-you free-wealth, and travel you shopping-travelling there to lands, as you wish".	"Then I give to you free wealth and you may travel and purchase there lands as you wish".
Hann lézt eigi þat vildu.	He had not that willed.	He said that he did not wish for this.
Þá mælti konungr:	Then said the-king:	Then the king said:
"Vandast mér nú heldr, því at eftir hefi ek nú leitat sem ek kann.	"Difficult for-me now rather, because that after have I now sought that-which I can.	"This is rather difficult for me now after I have sought all that I can.
Ok er nú einn eftir hlutrinn, ok er sá alllítils verðr hjá þessum, er ek hefi boðit þér, en þó kann eigi geta, hvat helzt hlýðir.	And is it now one after thing, and is so little worth next-to these, that I have offered to-you, but though know not get, what preferably obeys.	And now there is one thing after that is of little worth next to these that I have offered to you, but though one can not know what is best".
Far þú nú hvern dag, þá er borð eru uppi, á fund minn, ok ek sitk eigi um nauðsynjamálum, ok mun ek hjala við þik.	Travel you now each day, then to tables they-are up, to find mine, and I sit not about needful-matters, and shall I talk with you.	"You shall travel each day then to my tables when they are up to find me, when I am not sitting on needful matters, and I shall talk with you.
Skulum vit ræða um konu þessa alla vega, þess er þú [vill] ok má í hug koma, ok mun ek gefa mér tóm til þessa, því at þat verðr stundum, at mönnum verðr harms síns at léttara, er um er rætt.	We-shall with discuss about woman this all ways, this that you wish and may to thought come, and shall I give myself time to this, accordingly that it becomes awhile, that men becomes sorrow theirs that lightened, are about is discussed.	We-shall with discuss about this woman all ways that you wish and may come to mind, and shall I give myself time to this accordingly, that it becomes after a while that men's sorrow becomes lightened when it is talked about.
Ok þat skal ok þessu fylgja, at aldri skaltu gjaflaust í brott fara frá mínum fundi".	And that shall and this follow, that never shall-you giftless to away travel from my meeting".	And this shall follow, that you shall never travel away from my meeting without a gift".
Ívarr svaraði:	Ivar answered:	Ivar answered:
"Þetta vil ek, herra, ok haf þökk fyrir eftirleitunina".	"That will I, lord, and have thanks for after-seeking".	"That I wish for lord, and I have thanks for your consideration".

The Tale of Ívarr Son of Ingimundr (Old Norse)

Old Norse	Literal	English
Ok nú gera þeir svá, at jafnan, er konungr sitr eigi yfir vandamálum, þá talar hann oft um þessa konu við Ívar.	And now did they so, to equally, and the-king sat not over problems, then talk he often about this woman with Ivar.	And now they did so, equally the king sat over problems, and then talked often about this woman with Ivar.
Ok þetta hlýddi bragðit, ok bættist nú Ívari harms síns vánum bráðara.	And this followed looked, and improved now Ivar's grief his hoped sooner-than.	And so it followed, that it looked that now to Ivar that his grief improved sonner than he had hoped.
Gladdist hann eftir þetta, ok kemr í samt lag sem fyrr hafði verit um skemmtun hans ok gleði.	Gladdest he after this, and came to same place as before had been about amusement his and gladness.	Gladdened was he after this, and it came to the same as it was before, his amusement and gladness.
Ok er hann með Eysteini.	And was he with Eystein.	And he remained with Eystein.

Word List (Old Norse to English)

Word List (Old Norse to English)

Old Norse	English	*Old Norse*	English
## *A, a*		## *D, d*	
af	of, off	*dag*	day
aftr	back	*draga*	drag
aldri	never	*dýrðarmaðr*	glorious-man
alla	all		
alllítils	little	## *E, e*	
allra	of-all		
annarr	another	*eða*	and, or
at	by, from, of, that, to	*ef*	if
		eftir	after
## *Á, á*		*eftirleitunina*	after-seeking
		eftirsjá	look-back
á	has, that, to	*eigi*	none, not, owns
áðr	before	*eignum*	owning
ástmenn	beloved-friends	*eigu*	posess
ástsamliga	affectionate	*eigur*	ownership
		einhverja	one
## *Æ, æ*		*einn*	one
		ek	I
æ	ever	*ekki*	not
ætt	ancestry	*en*	but, that
		engi	no
## *B, b*		*engu*	none
		er	and, are, as, going, has, if, is, is it, it-is, that, to, was, when, who
bað	ask		
bættist	improved		
bauð	offered		
bera	carry		
biði	wait-for	*ertu*	you-are
bjóst	prepare	*eru*	are, are-there, is-there, they-are
boðit	offered		
borð	tables	*Eysteini*	Eystein (name)
bráðara	sooner-than	*Eysteinn*	Eystein (name)
bræðr	brothers	*Eysteins*	Eystein (name)
bragðit	looked		
bréf	letters	## *F, f*	
bróðir	brother		
bróður	brother	*fá*	get, give
brott	away	*fæ*	give
		fagrar	fair
		fann	found

Word List (Old Norse to English)

Old Norse	English
far	travel
fara	travel
farit	the-matter
fé	wealth
fekk	married
ferr	travel, travelled
fór	travelled
forræði	authority, power
frá	from, of
framar	from
fund	find, meet
fundi	meeting
fundizt	found
fylgja	follow
fyrir	for
fyrr	before

G, g

Old Norse	English
gefa	give
gera	did
gert	done
geta	get, guess
getan	guessing
getist	estimate
gifta	give-in-marriage
giftist	be-married
gjaflaust	gitfless
gladdist	gladdest
gleði	gladness
góðu	good
gott	good
grun	suspicion

H, h

Old Norse	English
haf	have
hafa	have, having, to-have
hafði	had
haft	had
hana	her
handa	hand
hann	he, he-was, him
hans	he, him, his
harmi	grief
harmr	grief
harms	grief, sorrow
hefi	have
hefir	have
heimtí	summoned
heldr	rather
helzt	preferably
hennar	her
hér	here
herra	lord
hét	named, was-named
hjá	next-to
hjala	talk
hlut	matter, part
hluti	things
hlutrinn	thing
hlýddi	followed
hlýðir	obeys
höfum	have
hon	she
honum	he, him
hug	thought
hugkvæmr	thoughtful
hugsjúkr	mind-sick
hvat	that, what
hve	how
hverfum	let-us-go
hvern	each
hverr	who
hví	why

I, i

Old Norse	English
illa	bad
Ingimundarson	son-of-Ingimundur (name)
innsigli	royal-seal

Í, í

Word List (Old Norse to English)

Old Norse	English
í	in, to
Íslands	Iceland (place)
íslenzkr	Icelander
Ívar	Ivar (name)
Ívari	Ivar's (name)
Ívarr	Ivar (name)
Ívars	Ivar's (name)

J, j

Old Norse	English
jafnan	equally
jafnmenni	equal-to
Jóansdóttur	Joansdottir (name)
jólin	Yule

K, k

Old Norse	English
kann	can, know
kaupferðir	shopping-travelling
kemr	came
kom	came
koma	come
komit	become
konar	kinds-of
konu	woman
konuna	a-wife, this-woman
konungbornar	kings-born
konungi	the-king
konungr	king, the-king
konungs	the-king
konur	woman, women
kurteisar	polite
kveðr	said
kvenna	women
kyni	kin

L, l

Old Norse	English
lag	place
landa	lands
landi	land
landinu	the-land
lausafé	free-wealth
leita	asking, seek
leitat	sought
lét	had
léttara	lightened
lézt	had
litlu	a-little

M, m

Old Norse	English
má	may, may-be
maðr	man
mæla	say
mælti	said
máli	matter
málinu	lord
máls	speak
manna	men, people's
margar	many
margs	many
marka	marked
með	with
meiri	greater
menn	man
mér	for-me, me, myself, to-me
mest	the-most
mik	mine
mikils	much
mikit	greatly, much
mikla	much
minn	mine, my
minna	less
minnir	memory
mínu	my
minum	my
mitt	mine
mjök	much
mönnum	men
mörgum	many
mun	shall, should
muntu	shall, should-you

N, n

Word List (Old Norse to English)

Old Norse	English
ná	get
nauðsynjamálum	needful-matters
naut	enjoyed
neitti	nothing
njóta	enjoy
nökkur	any, some
nökkura	any
nökkurar	some
nökkurir	some
nökkurum	anything
nú	now

O, o

Old Norse	English
Oddnýjar	Oddny (name)
Oddnýju	Oddynja (name)
oft	often
ok	and
orð	word
orðum	words
oss	ours, us

Ó, ó

Old Norse	English
ógleði	sadness
ógnarorðum	menacing-words
ókátr	displeased
ór	of

R, r

Old Norse	English
ráð	advise, decision
ráða	power
ræða	discuss
rætt	discussed
reiðfari	travelled

S, s

Old Norse	English
sá	so, that
samt	same
sé	say, see, yourself
seg	say
segir	said
segja	say
sem	as, that-which, which
sér	he, her
sét	seen
síðan	afterwards, then
síðar	later
sik	him
sína	his
síns	his, theirs
sitk	sit
sitr	sat
sjá	see
skal	shall
skáld	poet
skaltu	shall-you
skemmtan	amusement
skemmtir	amuse
skemmtun	amusement
skilðist	parted
skulum	we-shall
skyldi	should
sóma	honour
spurði	asked
stórættaðr	large-family
stundum	awhile
svá	so, such
svaraði	answered
sýnist	seems

T, t

Old Norse	English
talar	talk
tekr	took
til	to
tók	took
tóm	time

Þ, þ

Old Norse	English
þá	then

Word List (Old Norse to English)

Old Norse	English
þær	therefore
þangat	there
þar	here, there, there, therefore
þat	it, that, the
þau	then
þegar	as-soon
þeim	theirs
þeima	that
þeir	they
þeira	they, those
þér	to-you, you, yourself
þess	this
þessa	this
þessar	this
þessu	this
þessum	these, this
þetta	that, this
þik	you
þó	nevertheless, though, yet
þökk	thanks
Þorfiðr	Thorfin (name), Thorfin (name)
Þorfinnr	Thorfin (name), Thorfin (name)
þótti	thought, thought
þú	to-you, you
þungligar	is, the-heavier
þurfa	needed
því	accordingly, because, since, such, that, therefore
þykkist	seeming
þykkja	be-valued

U, u

um	about, about-it
unði	part
uni	like
unir	satisfied
uppi	up

Ú, ú

út	out
útan	out

V, v

væri	was
vandamálum	problems
vandast	difficult
vánir	hopes
vánum	hoped
var	was, were
várar	spring
varð	was
váruð	were
várum	our
veg	way
vega	ways
veit	know
veizlur	feasts
vel	well
ver	be
vér	we
vera	be, being, was
verðr	becomes, worth
verit	been
við	with
víkja	give-in
vil	will, wish
vildir	wish
vildu	willed
vill	wish
villtu	will-you
vinhollr	friend-whole
vinmælum	friendly-words
virði	worthed
vit	with
vita	knew
vitr	wise

Y, y

yðru	your
yðrum	your

Word List (Old Norse to English)

Old Norse   English

yfir   over
yfirlæti   favour

Word List (English to Old Norse)

Word List (English to Old Norse)

English	Old Norse
A, a	
about	um
about-it	um
accordingly	því
advise	ráð
affectionate	ástsamliga
after	eftir
after-seeking	eftirleitunina
afterwards	síðan
a-little	litlu
all	alla
amuse	skemmtir
amusement	skemmtan, skemmtun
ancestry	ætt
and	eða, er, ok
another	annarr
answered	svaraði
any	nökkur, nökkura
anything	nökkurum
are	er, eru
are-there	eru
as	er, sem
ask	bað
asked	spurði
asking	leita
as-soon	þegar
authority	forræði
away	brott
awhile	stundum
a-wife	konuna
B, b	
back	aftr
bad	illa
be	ver, vera
because	því
become	komit
becomes	verðr
been	verit
before	áðr, fyrr

English	Old Norse
being	vera
beloved-friends	ástmenn
be-married	giftist
be-valued	þykkja
brother	bróðir, bróður
brothers	bræðr
but	en
by	at
C, c	
came	kemr, kom
can	kann
carry	bera
come	koma
D, d	
day	dag
decision	ráð
did	gera
difficult	vandast
discuss	ræða
discussed	rætt
displeased	ókátr
done	gert
drag	draga
E, e	
each	hvern
enjoy	njóta
enjoyed	naut
equally	jafnan
equal-to	jafnmenni
estimate	getist
ever	æ
Eystein (name)	Eysteini, Eysteinn, Eysteins
F, f	

Word List (English to Old Norse)

English	Old Norse
fair	fagrar
favour	yfirlæti
feasts	veizlur
find	fund
follow	fylgja
followed	hlýddi
for	fyrir
for-me	mér
found	fann, fundizt
free-wealth	lausafé
friendly-words	vinmælum
friend-whole	vinhollr
from	at, frá, framar

G, g

get	fá, geta, ná
gitfless	gjaflaust
give	fá, fæ, gefa
give-in	víkja
give-in-marriage	gifta
gladdest	gladdist
gladness	gleði
glorious-man	dýrðarmaðr
going	er
good	góðu, gott
greater	meiri
greatly	mikit
grief	harmi, harmr, harms
guess	geta
guessing	getan

H, h

had	hafði, haft, lét, lézt
hand	handa
has	á, er
have	haf, hafa, hefi, hefir, höfum
having	hafa
he	hann, hans, honum, sér
her	hana, hennar, sér

English	Old Norse
here	hér, þar
he-was	hann
him	hann, hans, honum, sik
his	hans, sína, síns
honour	sóma
hoped	vánum
hopes	vánir
how	hve

I, i

I	ek
Iceland (place)	Íslands
Icelander	íslenzkr
if	ef, er
improved	bættist
in	í
is	er, þungligar
is it	er
is-there	eru
it	þat
it-is	er
Ivar (name)	Ívar, Ívarr
Ivar's (name)	Ívari, Ívars

J, j

Joansdottir (name)	Jóansdóttur

K, k

kin	kyni
kinds-of	konar
king	konungr
kings-born	konungbornar
knew	vita
know	kann, veit

L, l

land	landi

Word List (English to Old Norse)

English	Old Norse	English	Old Norse
lands	landa	no	engi
large-family	stórættaðr	none	eigi, engu
later	síðar	not	eigi, ekki
less	minna	nothing	neitti
letters	bréf	now	nú
let-us-go	hverfum		
lightened	léttara		
like	uni		
little	alllítils		
look-back	eftirsjá		
looked	bragðit		
lord	herra, málinu		

O, o

English	Old Norse
obeys	hlýðir
Oddny (name)	Oddnýjar
Oddynja (name)	Oddnýju
of	af, at, frá, ór
of-all	allra
off	af
offered	bauð, boðit
often	oft
one	einhverja, einn
or	eða
our	várum
ours	oss
out	út, útan
over	yfir
ownership	eigur
owning	eignum
owns	eigi

M, m

English	Old Norse
man	maðr, menn
many	margar, margs, mörgum
marked	marka
married	fekk
matter	hlut, máli
may	má
may-be	má
me	mér
meet	fund
meeting	fundi
memory	minnir
men	manna, mönnum
menacing-words	ógnarorðum
mind-sick	hugsjúkr
mine	mik, minn, mitt
much	mikils, mikit, mikla, mjök
my	minn, mínu, minum
myself	mér

P, p

English	Old Norse
part	hlut, unði
parted	skilðist
people's	manna
place	lag
poet	skáld
polite	kurteisar
posess	eigu
power	forræði, ráða
preferably	helzt
prepare	bjóst
problems	vandamálum

N, n

English	Old Norse
named	hét
needed	þurfa
needful-matters	nauðsynjamálum
never	aldri
nevertheless	þó
next-to	hjá

R, r

English	Old Norse
rather	heldr

Word List (English to Old Norse)

English	Old Norse	*English*	Old Norse
royal-seal	innsigli	*that-which*	sem
		the	þat
		the-heavier	þungligar
		theirs	síns, þeim
		the-king	konungi, konungr, konungs

S, s

		the-land	landinu
sadness	ógleði	*the-matter*	farit
said	kveðr, mælti, segir	*the-most*	mest
same	samt	*then*	síðan, þá, þau
sat	sitr	*there*	þangat, þar, þar
satisfied	unir	*therefore*	þær, þar, því
say	mæla, sé, seg, segja	*these*	þessum
see	sé, sjá	*they*	þeir, þeira
seek	leita	*they-are*	eru
seeming	þykkist	*thing*	hlutrinn
seems	sýnist	*things*	hluti
seen	sét	*this*	þess, þessa, þessar, þessu, þessum, þetta
shall	mun, muntu, skal		
shall-you	skaltu		
she	hon	*this-woman*	konuna
shopping-travelling	kaupferðir	*Thorfin (name)*	Þorfiðr, Þorfiðr, Þorfinnr, Þorfinnr
should	mun, skyldi		
should-you	muntu	*those*	þeira
since	því	*though*	þó
sit	sitk	*thought*	hug, þótti, þótti
so	sá, svá	*thoughtful*	hugkvæmr
some	nökkur, nökkurar, nökkurir	*time*	tóm
		to	á, at, er, í, til
son-of-Ingimundur (name)	Ingimundarson	*to-have*	hafa
		to-me	mér
sooner-than	bráðara	*took*	tekr, tók
sorrow	harms	*to-you*	þér, þú
sought	leitat	*travel*	far, fara, ferr
speak	máls	*travelled*	ferr, fór, reiðfari
spring	várar		
such	svá, því		
summoned	heimtí		
suspicion	grun		

U, u

up	uppi
us	oss

T, t

tables	borð
talk	hjala, talar
thanks	þökk
that	á, at, en, er, hvat, sá, þat, þeima, þetta, því

W, w

wait-for	biði

Word List (English to Old Norse)

English	Old Norse
was	er, væri, var, varð, vera
was-named	hét
way	veg
ways	vega
we	vér
wealth	fé
well	vel
were	var, váruð
we-shall	skulum
what	hvat
when	er
which	sem
who	er, hverr
why	hví
will	vil
willed	vildu
will-you	villtu
wise	vitr
wish	vil, vildir, vill
with	með, við, vit
woman	konu, konur
women	konur, kvenna
word	orð
words	orðum
worth	verðr
worthed	virði

Y, y

yet	þó
you	þér, þik, þú
you-are	ertu
your	yðru, yðrum
yourself	sé, þér
Yule	jólin

The Tale of Ívarr Son of Ingimundr (*Old Icelandic*)

Old Icelandic	Literal	English
Í þeima hlut má marka er nú mun eg segja hver dýrðarmaður Eysteinn konungur var eða hve mjög hann var vinhollur og hugkvæmur eftir að leita við sína ástmenn hvað þeim væri að harmi.	In that part may-be marked that now shall I say who glorious-man Eystein king was and how much he was friend-whole and thoughtful after to seek with his beloved-friends that theirs was of grief.	In part it may be said that I shall now say who the glorious king Eystein was and how much he was a good friend and thoughtful in seeking with his beloved friends what was their grief.
Sá maður var með Eysteini konungi er Ívar hét og var Ingimundarson, íslenskur að ætt og stórættaður að kyni, vitur maður og skáld gott.	That man was with Eystein the-king was Ivar named and was Son-of-Ingimundur, Icelander by ancestry and large-family to kin, wise man and poet good.	That man was with Eystein the king and was named Ivar and he was the son of Ingimundur, an Icelander by ancestry with a large family and kin, a wise man and a good poet.
Konungur virti hann mikils og var til hans ástsamlega sem sýnist í þessum hlut.	The-king worthed him much and was to him affectionate as seems in this matter.	The king valued him very much and was affectionate to him as it seems in this matter.
Þorfinnur hét bróðir Ívars.	Thorfin was-named brother Ivar's.	Ivar's brother was named Thorfin.
Hann fór og utan á fund Eysteins konungs og naut þar mjög frá mörgum mönnum bróður síns.	He travelled and out to meet Eystein the-king and enjoyed there much from many men brother his.	He travelled out to meet Eystein the king and enjoyed much of his brother's popularity with many men there.
En honum þótti það mikið er hann skyldi eigi þykja jafnmenni bróður síns og þurfa hans að njóta og undi af því eigi með konungi og bjóst út til Íslands.	But he thought it much that he should not be-valued equal-to brother his and needed he to enjoy and part off therefore not with the-king and prepare out to Iceland.	But he thought it was a bit much that he was not valued as equal to his brother, on whom he depended for that which he enjoyed, and therefore parted with the king and prepared to travel out to Iceland.
Og áður en þeir bræður skildust mælti Ívar að Þorfinnur skyldi þau orð bera Oddnýju Jóansdóttur að hún biði hans og giftist eigi, lét sér um hana mest vera allra kvenna.	And before that they brothers parted said Ivar that Thorfin should then word carry Oddnyja Joansdottir that she wait-for him and be-married not, had he about her the-most being of-all women.	And before the brothers parted Ivar said that Thorfin should carry word to Oddynja Joansdottir for her to wait for him and not marry, for he held her above all other women.
Síðan fer Þorfinnur út og varð vel reiðfari og tók það ráð að hann bað Oddnýjar sér til handa og fékk hennar.	Then travelled Thorfin out and was well travelled and took the decision that he ask Oddny her to hand and married her.	Then Thorfin fared out and travelled well, and he decided to ask Oddyn for her hand in marriage himself.

The Tale of Ívarr Son of Ingimundr (Old Icelandic)

Old Icelandic	Literal	English
Og litlu síðar kom Ívar út og frá þetta og þótti Þorfinnur illa hafa úr haft við sig og unir hann öngu og fer aftur síðan til konungs og er með honum í góðu yfirlæti sem fyrr.	And a-little later came Ivar out and of this and thought Thorfin bad having of had with him and satisfied he-was none and travelled back afterwards to the-king and was with him in good favour as before.	And a little later Ivar came out to Iceland and heard about this, and thought that Thorfin had done bad to him, and he was most unsatisfied, and travelled back to the king and was held in good favour with him as before.
Ívar tekur nú ógleði mikla og er konungur fann það heimti hann Ívar til máls við sig og spurði hví hann væri svo ókátur og fyrr er þér voruð með oss var margs konar skemmtan að yðrum orðum.	Ivar took now sadness much and as the-king found it summoned he Ivar to speak with him and asked why he was so displeased and before when you were with us were many kinds-of amusement from your words.	Ivar took to a great sadness and when the king noticed he summoned Ivar to speak with him and asked him why he was so displeased "Whereas before when you were with us, there was much amusement from your words.
Og eigi leita eg fyrir því eftir þessu að eigi viti eg að vér höfum ekki af gert við þig.	And not asking I for since after this that not knew I that we have not of done with you.	And I do not ask since we do know know if it is because we have wronged you.
Ertu og svo vitur maður að eigi muntu grun draga af því er eigi er og seg mér hvað er.	You-are and such wise man that not should-you suspicion drag of therefore if not is and say to-me what is.	For you are such a wise man that you would not suspect a slight where none exists, and please tell me what it is".
Ívar svaraði:	Ivar answered:	Ivar answered:
"Það sem er herra má eg ekki frá segja.	"That which is lord may I not from say".	"What it is lord I may not say".
Konungur mælti:	The-King said:	The king said:
"Eg mun þá geta til.	"I should then guess to	"Then I should gess it.
Eru nokkurir menn þeir er þér getist eigi að?	Is-there some man they who to-you estimate not of?"	Is there some man who you do not hold in esteem?"
Eigi er það herra, segir Ívar.	Not is that lord, said Ivar.	"It is not that, lord", said Ivar.
Konungur mælti:	The-King said:	The king said:
"Þykist þú af mér hafa minna sóma en þú vildir?	"Seeming to-you of me have less honour that you wish?"	"Do you think of me that I have less honour than you wish?".
"Eigi er það herra, segir hann.	"Not is that lord, said he.	"It is not that, lord", said he.

The Tale of Ívarr Son of Ingimundr (Old Icelandic)

Old Icelandic	Literal	English
"Hefir þú séð nokkura hluti, segir konungur, "þá er þér hafa svo mikið um fundist hér í landinu?	"Have you seen any things, said the-king, "then that to-you have so greatly about found here in the-land?"	"Have you seen anything", said the king, "that you have found in this land which you covet?".
Hann kveður eigi það vera.	He said not that was.	He said that it was not that.
"Vandast oss nú getan, segir konungur.	"Difficult ours now guessing, said the-king.	"It is now difficult for us to guess", said the king.
"Viltu hafa forræði nokkur yfir eignum nokkurum?	"Will-you to-have power any over owning anything?"	"Do you wish to have authority over or some ownership of something?".
Hann neitti því.	He nothing such.	He said it was nothing as such.
"Eru nokkurar konur þær á yðru landi, segir konungur, "er þér sé eftirsjá að?	"Are-there some woman therefore that your land" said the-king, "that you yourself look-back to?"	"Are there any women there in your land", said the king, "that you look back to with regret?".
Hann svaraði:	He answered:	He answered:
"Svo er herra.	"So it-is lord".	"So it is, lord".
Konungur mælti:	The-King said:	The king said:
"Ver eigi þar um hugsjúkur.	"Be not therefore about-it mind-sick.	"Therefore do not be anxious about it.
Þegar er vorar far þú út.	As-soon as spring travel you out.	As soon as the spring comes you shall travel out.
Mun eg fá þér fé og bréf mitt með innsigli til þeirra manna er ráða eiga og veit eg eigi þeirra manna vonir að eigi víkja eftir vorum vinmælum eða ógnarorðum að gifta konuna.	Shall I give you wealth and letters mine with royal-seal to those men who power posess and know I not they people's hopes that not give-in after our friendly-words or menacing-words to give-in-marriage this-woman".	I shall give you wealth and letters with a royal seal to those men who have the authority, and I do not know of anyone who will not give in after our friendly words or menacing words to give this woman in marriage".
Ívar svaraði:	Ivar answered:	Ivar answered:
"Eigi má svo vera.	"Not may so be".	"It may not be so".
Konungur mælti:	The-King said:	The king said:

The Tale of Ívarr Son of Ingimundr (Old Icelandic)

Old Icelandic	Literal	English
"Engi veg má þess vera, segir konungur.	"No way may this be, said the-king.	"There is no way this may be", said the king.
"Því mun eg mæla framar þó að annar maður eigi hana þá mun eg þó ná ef eg vil þér til handa.	"Therefore shall I say from yet that another man owns her then shall I nevertheless get if I wish you to hand".	"Therefore I shall say that yet another man owns her, then I shall nevertheless get her if you wish for her hand".
Ívar svaraði:	Ivar answered:	Ivar answered:
"Þunglegar er farið málinu herra.	"Difficult is going the-matter lord.	"This is where the matter becomes difficult, lord.
Bróðir minn á nú konuna.	Brother mine has now a-wife".	My brother now has her as a wife".
Þá mælti konungur:	Then said the-king:	Then the king said:
"Hverfum þar frá, segir hann.	"Let-us-go here from, said he.	"Then let us go from here", he said.
"Sé eg þá ráð til.	"Say I then advise to.	"I say then to advise.
Eftir jólin mun eg fara á veislur og far þú með mér og muntu þar sjá margar kurteisar konur og ef eigi eru konungbornar þá mun eg fá þér einhverja.	After Yule shall I travel to feasts and travel you with me and shall there see many polite women and if none are kings-born then shall I get you one".	After Yule I shall travel to feasts and you shall travel with me and you shall see there many polite women, and if there are no kings born, then I shall get you one".
Ívar svaraði:	Ivar answered:	Ivar answered:
"Herra, því þunglegar er komið mínu máli að jafnan er eg sé fagrar konur þá minnir mig þessar konu og er æ því meiri minn harmur.	"Lord, because the-heavier has become my matter to equally that I see fair woman then memory mine this woman and is ever therefore greater my grief"	"Lord, because my matter has become heavier, equally when I see a fair woman then I have memory of this woman, and my grief is ever therefore greater".
Konungur mælti:	The-King said:	The king said:
"Þá mun eg gefa þér nokkur forræði og eigur sem eg bauð þér fyrr og skemmtir þú þér við það.	"Then shall I give to-you some authority and ownership which I offered you before and amuse you yourself with that".	"Then I shall give to you some authority and ownership which I offered you before and you can amuse yourself with that".
Hann svaraði:	He answered:	He answered:

The Tale of Ívarr Son of Ingimundr (Old Icelandic)

Old Icelandic	Literal	English
"Ekki uni eg því.	"Not like I that".	"I do not like that".
Konungur mælti:	The-King said:	The king said:
"Þá fæ eg þér lausafé og ferð þú kaupferðir þangað til landa sem þú vilt.	"Then give I to-you free-wealth and travel you shopping-travelling there to lands as you wish".	"Then I give to you free wealth and you may travel and purchase there lands as you wish".
Hann lést eigi það vildu.	He had not that willed.	He said that he did not wish for this.
Þá mælti konungur:	Then said the-king:	Then the king said:
"Vandast mér nú heldur því að eftir hefi eg nú leitað sem eg kann.	"Difficult for-me now rather because that after have I now sought that-which I can	"This is rather difficult for me now after I have sought all that I can.
Og er nú einn eftir hluturinn og er sá alllítils verður hjá þessum er eg hefi boðið þér en þó kann eigi geta hvað helst hlýðir.	And is it now one after thing and is so little worth next-to these that I have offered to-you but though know not get what preferably obeys".	And now there is one thing after that is of little worth next to these that I have offered to you, but though one can not know what is best".
"Far þú nú hvern dag þá er borð eru uppi á fund minn og eg sit eigi um nauðsynjamálum og mun eg hjala við þig.	"Travel you now each day then to tables they-are up to find mine and I sit not about needful-matters and shall I talk with you	"You shall travel each day then to my tables when they are up to find me, when I am not sitting on needful matters, and I shall talk with you.
Skulum við ræða um konu þessa alla vega þess er þú vilt og má í hug koma og mun eg gefa mér tóm til þessa því að það verður stundum að mönnum verður harms síns að léttara er um er rætt.	We-shall with discuss about woman this all ways this that you wish and may to thought come and shall I give myself time to this accordingly that it becomes awhile that men becomes sorrow theirs that lightened are about is discussed.	We-shall with discuss about this woman all ways that you wish and may come to mind, and shall I give myself time to this accordingly, that it becomes after a while that men's sorrow becomes lightened when it is talked about.
Og það skal og þessu fylgja að aldrei skaltu gjaflaust í brott fara frá mínum fundi.	And that shall and this follow that never shall-you giftless to away travel from my meeting".	And this shall follow, that you shall never travel away from my meeting without a gift".
Ívar svaraði:	Ivar answered:	Ivar answered:
"Þetta vil eg herra og haf þökk fyrir eftirleituna.	"That will I lord and have thanks for after-seeking".	"That I wish for lord, and I have thanks for your consideration".

The Tale of Ívarr Son of Ingimundr (Old Icelandic)

Old Icelandic	Literal	English
Og nú gera þeir svo að jafnan er konungur situr eigi yfir vandamálum þá talar hann oft um þessa konu við Ívar.	And now did they so to equally and the-king sat not over problems then talk he often about this woman with Ivar.	And now they did so, equally the king sat over problems, and then talked often about this woman with Ivar.
Og þetta hlýddi bragðið og bættist nú Ívari harms síns vonum bráðara.	And this followed looked and improved now Ivar's grief his hoped sooner-than.	And so it followed, that it looked that now to Ivar that his grief improved sonner than he had hoped.
Gladdist hann eftir þetta og kemur í samt lag sem fyrr hafði verið um skemmtun hans og gleði.	Gladdest he after this and came to same place as before had been about amusement his and gladness.	Gladdened was he after this, and it came to the same as it was before, his amusement and gladness.
Og er hann með Eysteini.	And was he with Eystein.	And he remained with Eystein.

Word List (Old Icelandic to English)

Word List (Old Icelandic to English)

Old Icelandic	English	*Old Icelandic*	English

A, a

að	by, from, of, that, to
af	of, off
aftur	back
aldrei	never
alla	all
alllítils	little
allra	of-all
annar	another

Á, á

á	has, that, to
áður	before
ástmenn	beloved-friends
ástsamlega	affectionate

Æ, æ

æ	ever
ætt	ancestry

B, b

bað	ask
bættist	improved
bauð	offered
bera	carry
biði	wait-for
bjóst	prepare
boðið	offered
borð	tables
bráðara	sooner-than
bræður	brothers
bragðið	looked
bréf	letters
bróðir	brother
bróður	brother
brott	away

D, d

dag	day
draga	drag
dýrðarmaður	glorious-man

E, e

eða	and, or
ef	if
eftir	after
eftirleituna	after-seeking
eftirsjá	look-back
eg	I
eiga	posess
eigi	none, not, owns
eignum	owning
eigur	ownership
einhverja	one
einn	one
ekki	not
en	but, that
engi	no
er	and, are, as, has, if, is, is it, it-is, that, to, was, when, who
ertu	you-are
eru	are, are-there, is-there, they-are
Eysteini	Eystein (name)
Eysteinn	Eystein (name)
Eysteins	Eystein (name)

F, f

fá	get, give
fæ	give
fagrar	fair
fann	found
far	travel
fara	travel

Word List (Old Icelandic to English)

Old Icelandic	English
farið	going
fé	wealth
fékk	married
fer	travelled
ferð	travel
fór	travelled
forræði	authority, power
frá	from, of
framar	from
fund	find, meet
fundi	meeting
fundist	found
fylgja	follow
fyrir	for
fyrr	before

G, g

Old Icelandic	English
gefa	give
gera	did
gert	done
geta	get, guess
getan	guessing
getist	estimate
gifta	give-in-marriage
giftist	be-married
gjaflaust	gitfless
gladdist	gladdest
gleði	gladness
góðu	good
gott	good
grun	suspicion

H, h

Old Icelandic	English
haf	have
hafa	have, having, to-have
hafði	had
haft	had
hana	her
handa	hand
hann	he, he-was, him
hans	he, him, his
harmi	grief
harms	grief, sorrow
harmur	grief
hefi	have
hefir	have
heimti	summoned
heldur	rather
helst	preferably
hennar	her
hér	here
herra	lord
hét	named, was-named
hjá	next-to
hjala	talk
hlut	matter, part
hluti	things
hluturinn	thing
hlýddi	followed
hlýðir	obeys
höfum	have
honum	he, him
hug	thought
hugkvæmur	thoughtful
hugsjúkur	mind-sick
hún	she
hvað	that, what
hve	how
hver	who
hverfum	let-us-go
hvern	each
hví	why

I, i

Old Icelandic	English
illa	bad
Ingimundarson	son-of-Ingimundur (name)
innsigli	royal-seal

Í, í

Old Icelandic	English
í	in, to
Íslands	Iceland (place)
íslenskur	Icelander
Ívar	Ivar (name)

Word List (Old Icelandic to English)

Old Icelandic	English
Ívari	Ivar's (name)
Ívars	Ivar's (name)

J, j

jafnan	equally
jafnmenni	equal-to
Jóansdóttur	Joansdottir (name)
jólin	Yule

K, k

kann	can, know
kaupferðir	shopping-travelling
kemur	came
kom	came
koma	come
komið	become
konar	kinds-of
konu	woman
konuna	a-wife, this-woman
konungbornar	kings-born
konungi	the-king
konungs	the-king
konungur	king, the-king
konur	woman, women
kurteisar	polite
kveður	said
kvenna	women
kyni	kin

L, l

lag	place
landa	lands
landi	land
landinu	the-land
lausafé	free-wealth
leita	asking, seek
leitað	sought
lést	had
lét	had
léttara	lightened
litlu	a-little

M, m

má	may, may-be
maður	man
mæla	say
mælti	said
máli	matter
málinu	the-matter
máls	speak
manna	men, people's
margar	many
margs	many
marka	marked
með	with
meiri	greater
menn	man
mér	for-me, me, myself, to-me
mest	the-most
mig	mine
mikið	greatly, much
mikils	much
mikla	much
minn	mine, my
minna	less
minnir	memory
mínu	my
mínum	my
mitt	mine
mjög	much
mönnum	men
mörgum	many
mun	shall, should
muntu	shall, should-you

N, n

ná	get
nauðsynjamálum	needful-matters
naut	enjoyed
neitti	nothing
njóta	enjoy

51

Word List (Old Icelandic to English)

Old Icelandic	English
nokkur	any, some
nokkura	any
nokkurar	some
nokkurir	some
nokkurum	anything
nú	now

O, o

Old Icelandic	English
Oddnýjar	Oddny (name)
Oddnýju	Oddynja (name)
oft	often
og	and
orð	word
orðum	words
oss	ours, us

Ó, ó

Old Icelandic	English
ógleði	sadness
ógnarorðum	menacing-words
ókátur	displeased

Ö, ö

Old Icelandic	English
öngu	none

R, r

Old Icelandic	English
ráð	advise, decision
ráða	power
ræða	discuss
rætt	discussed
reiðfari	travelled

S, s

Old Icelandic	English
sá	so, that
samt	same
sé	say, see, yourself
séð	seen
seg	say
segir	said
segja	say
sem	as, that-which, which
sér	he, her
síðan	afterwards, then
síðar	later
sig	him
sína	his
síns	his, theirs
sit	sit
situr	sat
sjá	see
skal	shall
skáld	poet
skaltu	shall-you
skemmtan	amusement
skemmtir	amuse
skemmtun	amusement
skildust	parted
skulum	we-shall
skyldi	should
sóma	honour
spurði	asked
stórættaður	large-family
stundum	awhile
svaraði	answered
svo	so, such
sýnist	seems

T, t

Old Icelandic	English
talar	talk
tekur	took
til	to
tók	took
tóm	time

Þ, þ

Old Icelandic	English
þá	then
það	it, that, the
þær	therefore
þangað	there

Word List (Old Icelandic to English)

Old Icelandic	English
þar	here, there, there, therefore
þau	then
þegar	as-soon
þeim	theirs
þeima	that
þeir	they
þeirra	they, those
þér	to-you, you, yourself
þess	this
þessa	this
þessar	this
þessu	this
þessum	these, this
þetta	that, this
þig	you
þó	nevertheless, though, yet
þökk	thanks
Þorfinnur	Thorfin (name), Thorfin (name)
þótti	thought, thought
þú	to-you, you
þunglegar	difficult, the-heavier
þurfa	needed
því	accordingly, because, since, such, that, therefore
þykist	seeming
þykja	be-valued

U, u

um	about, about-it
undi	part
uni	like
unir	satisfied
uppi	up
utan	out

Ú, ú

úr	of
út	out

V, v

Old Icelandic	English
væri	was
vandamálum	problems
vandast	difficult
var	was, were
varð	was
veg	way
vega	ways
veislur	feasts
veit	know
vel	well
ver	be
vér	we
vera	be, being, was
verður	becomes, worth
verið	been
við	with
víkja	give-in
vil	will, wish
vildir	wish
vildu	willed
vilt	wish
viltu	will-you
vinhollur	friend-whole
vinmælum	friendly-words
virti	worthed
viti	knew
vitur	wise
vonir	hopes
vonum	hoped
vorar	spring
voruð	were
vorum	our

Y, y

yðru	your
yðrum	your
yfir	over
yfirlæti	favour

Word List (English to Old Icelandic)

English	Old Icelandic
A, a	
about	um
about-it	um
accordingly	því
advise	ráð
affectionate	ástsamlega
after	eftir
after-seeking	eftirleituna
afterwards	síðan
a-little	litlu
all	alla
amuse	skemmtir
amusement	skemmtan, skemmtun
ancestry	ætt
and	eða, er, og
another	annar
answered	svaraði
any	nokkur, nokkura
anything	nokkurum
are	er, eru
are-there	eru
as	er, sem
ask	bað
asked	spurði
asking	leita
as-soon	þegar
authority	forræði
away	brott
awhile	stundum
a-wife	konuna
B, b	
back	aftur
bad	illa
be	ver, vera
because	því
become	komið
becomes	verður
been	verið
before	áður, fyrr
being	vera
beloved-friends	ástmenn
be-married	giftist
be-valued	þykja
brother	bróðir, bróður
brothers	bræður
but	en
by	að
C, c	
came	kemur, kom
can	kann
carry	bera
come	koma
D, d	
day	dag
decision	ráð
did	gera
difficult	þunglegar, vandast
discuss	ræða
discussed	rætt
displeased	ókátur
done	gert
drag	draga
E, e	
each	hvern
enjoy	njóta
enjoyed	naut
equally	jafnan
equal-to	jafnmenni
estimate	getist
ever	æ
Eystein (name)	Eysteini, Eysteinn, Eysteins
F, f	

Word List (English to Old Icelandic)

English	Old Icelandic
fair	fagrar
favour	yfirlæti
feasts	veislur
find	fund
follow	fylgja
followed	hlýddi
for	fyrir
for-me	mér
found	fann, fundist
free-wealth	lausafé
friendly-words	vinmælum
friend-whole	vinhollur
from	að, frá, framar

G, g

get	fá, geta, ná
gitfless	gjaflaust
give	fá, fæ, gefa
give-in	víkja
give-in-marriage	gifta
gladdest	gladdist
gladness	gleði
glorious-man	dýrðarmaður
going	farið
good	góðu, gott
greater	meiri
greatly	mikið
grief	harmi, harms, harmur
guess	geta
guessing	getan

H, h

had	hafði, haft, lést, lét
hand	handa
has	á, er
have	haf, hafa, hefi, hefir, höfum
having	hafa
he	hann, hans, honum, sér
her	hana, hennar, sér
here	hér, þar
he-was	hann
him	hann, hans, honum, sig
his	hans, sína, síns
honour	sóma
hoped	vonum
hopes	vonir
how	hve

I, i

I	eg
Iceland (place)	Íslands
Icelander	íslenskur
if	ef, er
improved	bættist
in	í
is	er
is it	er
is-there	eru
it	það
it-is	er
Ivar (name)	Ívar
Ivar's (name)	Ívari, Ívars

J, j

Joansdottir (name)	Jóansdóttur

K, k

kin	kyni
kinds-of	konar
king	konungur
kings-born	konungbornar
knew	viti
know	kann, veit

L, l

land	landi

Word List (English to Old Icelandic)

English	Old Icelandic
lands	landa
large-family	stórættaður
later	síðar
less	minna
letters	bréf
let-us-go	hverfum
lightened	léttara
like	uni
little	alllítils
look-back	eftirsjá
looked	bragðið
lord	herra

M, m

English	Old Icelandic
man	maður, menn
many	margar, margs, mörgum
marked	marka
married	fékk
matter	hlut, máli
may	má
may-be	má
me	mér
meet	fund
meeting	fundi
memory	minnir
men	manna, mönnum
menacing-words	ógnarorðum
mind-sick	hugsjúkur
mine	mig, minn, mitt
much	mikið, mikils, mikla, mjög
my	minn, mínu, mínum
myself	mér

N, n

English	Old Icelandic
named	hét
needed	þurfa
needful-matters	nauðsynjamálum
never	aldrei
nevertheless	þó
next-to	hjá
no	engi
none	eigi, öngu
not	eigi, ekki
nothing	neitti
now	nú

O, o

English	Old Icelandic
obeys	hlýðir
Oddny (name)	Oddnýjar
Oddynja (name)	Oddnýju
of	að, af, frá, úr
of-all	allra
off	af
offered	bauð, boðið
often	oft
one	einhverja, einn
or	eða
our	vorum
ours	oss
out	út, utan
over	yfir
ownership	eigur
owning	eignum
owns	eigi

P, p

English	Old Icelandic
part	hlut, undi
parted	skildust
people's	manna
place	lag
poet	skáld
polite	kurteisar
posess	eiga
power	forræði, ráða
preferably	helst
prepare	bjóst
problems	vandamálum

R, r

English	Old Icelandic
rather	heldur

Word List (English to Old Icelandic)

English	Old Icelandic
royal-seal	innsigli

S, s

English	Old Icelandic
sadness	ógleði
said	kveður, mælti, segir
same	samt
sat	situr
satisfied	unir
say	mæla, sé, seg, segja
see	sé, sjá
seek	leita
seeming	þykist
seems	sýnist
seen	séð
shall	mun, muntu, skal
shall-you	skaltu
she	hún
shopping-travelling	kaupferðir
should	mun, skyldi
should-you	muntu
since	því
sit	sit
so	sá, svo
some	nokkur, nokkurar, nokkurir
son-of-Ingimundur (name)	Ingimundarson
sooner-than	bráðara
sorrow	harms
sought	leitað
speak	máls
spring	vorar
such	svo, því
summoned	heimti
suspicion	grun

T, t

English	Old Icelandic
tables	borð
talk	hjala, talar
thanks	þökk
that	á, að, en, er, hvað, sá, það, þeima, þetta, því
that-which	sem
the	það
the-heavier	þunglegar
theirs	síns, þeim
the-king	konungi, konungs, konungur
the-land	landinu
the-matter	málinu
the-most	mest
then	síðan, þá, þau
there	þangað, þar
therefore	þær, þar, því
these	þessum
they	þeir, þeirra
they-are	eru
thing	hluturinn
things	hluti
this	þess, þessa, þessar, þessu, þessum, þetta
this-woman	konuna
Thorfin (name)	Þorfinnur
those	þeirra
though	þó
thought	hug, þótti
thoughtful	hugkvæmur
time	tóm
to	á, að, er, í, til
to-have	hafa
to-me	mér
took	tekur, tók
to-you	þér, þú
travel	far, fara, ferð
travelled	fer, fór, reiðfari

U, u

English	Old Icelandic
up	uppi
us	oss

W, w

Word List (English to Old Icelandic)

English	Old Icelandic
wait-for	biði
was	er, væri, var, varð, vera
was-named	hét
way	veg
ways	vega
we	vér
wealth	fé
well	vel
were	var, voruð
we-shall	skulum
what	hvað
when	er
which	sem
who	er, hver
why	hví
will	vil
willed	vildu
will-you	viltu
wise	vitur
wish	vil, vildir, vilt
with	með, við
woman	konu, konur
women	konur, kvenna
word	orð
words	orðum
worth	verður
worthed	virti

Y, y

yet	þó
you	þér, þig, þú
you-are	ertu
your	yðru, yðrum
yourself	sé, þér
Yule	jólin

A Word Comparison of Old Norse and Old Icelandic Words

A Word Comparison of Old Norse and Old Icelandic Words

Old Norse	Old Icelandic	English	Old Norse	Old Icelandic	English
áðr	áður	before	leitat	leitað	sought
aftr	aftur	back	lézt	lést	had
aldri	aldrei	never	maðr	maður	man
annarr	annar	another	mik	mig	mine
ástsamliga	ástsamlega	affectionate	mikit	mikið	greatly
at	að	by	mikit	mikið	much
at	að	from	minum	mínum	my
at	að	of	mjök	mjög	much
at	að	that	nökkur	nokkur	any
at	að	to	nökkur	nokkur	some
boðit	boðið	offered	nökkura	nokkura	any
bræðr	bræður	brothers	nökkurar	nokkurar	some
bragðit	bragðið	looked	nökkurir	nokkurir	some
dýrðarmaðr	dýrðarmaður	glorious-man	nökkurum	nokkurum	anything
eftirleitunina	eftirleituna	after-seeking	ok	og	and
eigu	eiga	posess	ókátr	ókátur	displeased
ek	eg	I	ór	úr	of
engu	öngu	none	sét	séð	seen
farit	farið	going	sik	sig	him
fekk	fékk	married	sitk	sit	sit
ferr	fer	travelled	sitr	situr	sat
ferr	ferð	travel	skilðist	skildust	parted
fundizt	fundist	found	stórættaðr	stórættaður	large-family
harmr	harmur	grief	svá	svo	so
heimtí	heimti	summoned	svá	svo	such
heldr	heldur	rather	tekr	tekur	took
helzt	helst	preferably	þangat	þangað	there
hlutrinn	hluturinn	thing	þat	það	it
hon	hún	she	þat	það	that
hugkvæmr	hugkvæmur	thoughtful	þat	það	the
hugsjúkr	hugsjúkur	mind-sick	þeira	þeirra	they
hvat	hvað	that	þeira	þeirra	those
hvat	hvað	what	þik	þig	you
hverr	hver	who	Þorfiðr	Þorfinnur	Thorfin (name)
íslenzkr	íslenskur	Icelander	Þorfinnr	Þorfinnur	Thorfin (name)
Ívarr	Ívar	Ivar (name)	þungligar	þunglegar	difficult
kemr	kemur	came	þungligar	þunglegar	the-heavier
komit	komið	become	þykkist	þykist	seeming
konungr	konungur	king	þykkja	þykja	be-valued
konungr	konungur	the-king	unði	undi	part
kveðr	kveður	said	útan	utan	out

A Word Comparison of Old Norse and Old Icelandic Words

Old Norse	Old Icelandic	English
vánir	vonir	hopes
vánum	vonum	hoped
várar	vorar	spring
váruð	voruð	were
várum	vorum	our
veizlur	veislur	feasts
verðr	verður	becomes
verðr	verður	worth
verit	verið	been
vill	vilt	wish
villtu	viltu	will-you
vinhollr	vinhollur	friend-whole
virði	virti	worthed
vit	við	with
vita	viti	knew
vitr	vitur	wise

The Tale of Thorstein Shiver (*Old Norse*)

Old Norse	Literal	English
1	**1**	**1**
Þat er sagt, um sumarit eftir, at Óláfr konungr fór at veizlum austr um Víkina ok víðara annars staðar..	It is said, about summer following, that Olaf the-king went to feasts east around Vik and wider other places..	It is said that the following summer, King Olaf went to feasts in the east around Vik and wider to other places.
Tók hann veizlu á þeim bæ, er á Reinu heitir..	Took he a-feast with them a-farm, which was Reim named..	He took a feast at a farm called Reim.
Hann var mjök fjölmennr..	He was-with many followers..	He was with many followers.
Sá var maðr þá með konungi, er Þorsteinn hét Þorkelsson, Ásgeirssonar æðikolls, Auðunarsonar skökuls, íslenzkr maðr, ok hafði komit til konungs um vetrinn áðr..	So was a-man there with the-king, who-was Thorstein named Son-of-Thorkel, Son-of-Asgeir rage-head, Son-of-Audun shaft, Icelandic man, and had come to the-king's about winter before..	Also there with the king was a man named Thorstein, the son of Thorkel, the son of Asgeir Rage-Head, son of Audun Shaft, an Icelander man, and he had come to the king around the winter before.
Um kveldit, er menn sátu yfir drykkjuborðum, talaði Óláfr konungr, at engi maðr af hans mönnum skyldi einn saman fara í salerni um náttina, því at hverr, sem ganga beiddist, skyldi með sér kalla sinn rekkjufélaga, ella kvað hann eigi mundu hlýða..	About evening, were the-men sitting over drinking-tables, told Olaf the-king, that no man of his men should alone together go to toilet about night-time, therefore that each, who go ask, should with them call their bed-fellow, or-else be-called him not will obey..	About evening, the men were sitting at the drinking tables, and Olaf the king made a speech, that none of his men should go alone to the toilet during the night, and that anyone who must go, should ask their bed fellow to accompany them, or they will have disobeyed him.
Drekka menn nú vel um kveldit, en er ofan váru drykkjuborð, gengu menn at sofa..	Drank the-men now well about the-evening, and when downed were drinking-tables, went men to sleep..	The men now drank well into the evening, and when the drinking tables were taken down, the men went to sleep.
Ok er á leið náttina, vaknaði Þorsteinn íslendingr ok beiddi at ganga af sæng, en sá svaf fast, er hjá honum lá, svá at Þorsteinn vildi víst eigi vekja hann..	And when that during the-night, awoke Thorstein the-Icelander and needed to go from the-bed, but so slept fast, was beside him lay, so that Thorstein willed certainly not-to awake him..	And during the night, Thorstein the Icelander awoke and needed to go from his bed, but he who was beside him was fast asleep, so that Thorstein did not want to wake him.

The Tale of Thorstein Shiver (Old Norse)

Old Norse	Literal	English
Stendr hann þá upp ok kippir skóm á fætr sér ok tekr yfir sik einn feld þykkvan ok gengr til heimilishúss..	Stood he then up and drew his-shoes about feet his and took about himself a cloak thick and went to the-outhouse..	He then stood up, put his shoes on his feet, and drew a thick cloak around him, and went to the outhouse.
Þat var stórt hús, svá at ellifu menn máttu sitja hvárum megin..	It was a-large house, so that eleven men might sit each may..	It was a large outhouse, that might have fit eleven men sitting.
Sezt hann á yztu setu,	Sat he on the-outermost seat,	He sat on the outermost seat,
ok er hann hefir setit nökkura stund, sér hann, at púki kemr upp á innstu setu ok sat þar..	and as he had sat some while, saw he, that a-demon came up from the-innermost seat and sat there..	and as he sat there for a while, he saw that a demon came up from the innermost seat and sat there.
Þorsteinn mælti þá:.	Thorstein spoke then:.	Then Thorstein spoke:
"Hverr er þar kominn?"	"Who is that come?"	"Who is that there?"
Dólgrinn svarar:.	The-demon answered:.	The-demon answered:
"Hér er kominn Þorkell inn þunni, er fell á hræ með Haraldi konungi hilditönn"..	"Here is come Thorkel the thin, who fell about corpses with Harald the-king war-tooth".	"Here is Thorkel the Thin, who fell about corpses with king Harald Wartooth".
"Hvaðan kom þú nú at?"	"From-where came you now to?"	"Where did you come from?"
kvað Þorsteinn..	said Thorstein..	said Thorstein.
Hann sagðist nú nýkominn at ór helvíti..	He said now newly-come from out-of hell..	He said that he had newly come from hell.
"Hvat kanntu þaðan at segja?"	"What can-you of-there to say?"	"What can you tell me me about it there?"
spurði Þorsteinn..	asked Thorstein..	asked Thorstein.
Hinn svarar:.	He answered:.	He answered:
"Hvers villtu spyrja?".	"What will-you ask".	"What do you want to know?"
"Hverir þola bezt píslir í helvíti?".	"Who endures best the-torment in hell".	"Who endures the torments of hell best?"
"Engi betr",	"None better",	"There is none better...",

The Tale of Thorstein Shiver (Old Norse)

Old Norse	Literal	English
kvað púki,.	said the-demon,.	said the demon,
"en Sigurðr Fáfnisbani"..	"than Sigurd Fafnisbani".	"...than Sigurd Fafnisbani".
"Hverja písl hefir hann?".	"What torment has he".	"What torment does he have?"
"Hann kyndir ofn brennanda",	"He kindles the-oven burning",	"He kindles the oven burning",
sagði draugrinn..	said the-demon..	said the demon.
"Ekki þykkir mér þat svá mikil písl",	"Not seems to-me that so much torment",	"That does not seem to me to be such a torment",
segir Þorsteinn..	said Thorstein..	said Thorstein.
"Eigi er þat þó",	"Not is that though",	"It's not that though",
kvað púki,.	said the-demon,.	said the demon,
"því at hann er sjálfr kyndarinn"..	"because that he is himself the-kindling".	"Because he himself is the kindling".
"Mikit er þat þá",	"Much is that then",	"That is very much then",
kvað Þorsteinn,.	said Thorstein,.	said Thorstein.
"eða hverr þolir þar verst píslir?"	"but who endures there the-worst torment?"	"But who endures the worst torment?"
Draugrinn svarar:.	The-demon answered:.	The demon answered:
"Starkaðr inn gamli þolir verst, því at hann æpir svá, at oss fjöndunum er þat meiri pína en flest allt annat, svá at vér megum fyrir hans ópi aldri náðir hafa"..	"Starkad the old endures the-worst, because that he cries-out so, that to-us the-torment is that more torment than most all else, so that we may for his shrieking never mercy have".	"Starkad the Old endures it worst, because he cries out so much, that to us the torment is worse than anything else, so that we may have mercy from his shrieking".
"Hvat pínu hefir hann þess",	"What torment has he this",	"What torment does he have?...",
kvað Þorsteinn,.	said Thorstein,.	said Thorstein,
"er hann þolir svá illa, svá hraustr maðr sem hann hefir sagðr verit?".	"that he endures so badly, so brave a-man as he has-been said been".	"...that he endures it so badly, such a brave man as has been said to be?"

The Tale of Thorstein Shiver (Old Norse)

Old Norse	Literal	English
"Hann hefir öklaeld"..	"He has ankle-fire".	"He has fire up to his ankles".
"Ekki þykkir mér þat svá mikit",	"Not seems to-me that so much",	"That does not seem to me to be so much...",
sagði Þorsteirm,.	said Thorstein,.	said Thorstein,
"slíkum kappa sem hann hefir verit"..	"such hero as he has been".	"...such a hero as he has been".
"Ekki er þá rétt á litit",	"Not is that right all considered",	"Then you have not considered it all correctly...",
kvað draugr,.	said the-demon,.	said the demon,
"því at iljarnar einar standa upp ór eldinum"..	"because that soles-of-the-feet only stand above from the-flames".	"...because only the soles of his feet are sticking out from the flames".
"Mikit er þat",	"Much is that",	"That is a lot then",
kvað Þorsteinn,.	said Thorstein,.	said Thorstein,
"ok æp þú eftir honum nökkut óp"..	"and shriek you after him somehow cries-out".	"And now, shriek something like how he does, once".
"Þat skal vera",	"That shall be",	"So it shall be",
kvað púki..	said the-demon..	said the demon.
Hann sló þá í sundr á sér hváftunum ok setti upp gaul mikit, en Þorsteinn brá feldarskautinu at höfði sér..	He struck then to down of his cheeks and put up a-howl great, but Thorstein drew fur-cloak about head his..	He then threw open his jaws and put up a great howl, but Thorstein drew his fur cloak about his head.
Honum varð mjök ósvipt við óp þetta ok mælti:.	He was much un-thrown with shouting this and spoke:.	He remained unmoved at this shouting and spoke:
"Æpir hann þetta ópit mest svá?".	"Cries-out he this open mostly so".	"Is that the most he cries out?"
"Fjarri ferr um þat",	"Far away about that",	"Far from it...",
kvað draugr,.	said the-demon,.	said the demon,
"því at þetta er óp várt drýsildjöflanna"..	"because that this is shouting us petty-devils".	"...because that is the shouting of us petty devils".

The Tale of Thorstein Shiver (Old Norse)

Old Norse	Literal	English
"Æp þú eftir Starkaði lítt at", kvað Þorsteinn..	"Shriek you after Starkad a-little then", asked Thorstein..	"Shriek like Starkad does a little then", asked Thorstein.
"Þat má vel",	"That may well",	"So it shall be",
kvað púki..	said the-demon..	said the demon.
Tekr hann þá at æpa í annan tíma svá öskurliga, at Þorsteini þótti firn í, hversu mikit sjá fjandi, jafnlítill, gat gaulat..	Took he then to shrieking a second time so terribly, that Thorstein thought monstrous of, how-so great such a-fiend, as-small, could bellow..	He took to sheirking a second time so terribly, that Thorstein thought it was monstrous, that such a little fiend could bellow so loudly.
Þorsteinn gerir þá sem fyrr, at hann vafði feldinum at höfði sér, ok brá honum þó svá við, at ómegin var á honum, svá at hann vissi ekki til sín..	Thorstein did then as before, that he wrapped cloak about head his, and drew he then so against, that un-mighty was so he, so that he knew not to himself..	Thorstein then did as before, and wrapped his cloak around his head, but the shrieking paralysed him, and he fainted.
Þá spurði púkinn:.	Then asked the-demon:.	Then the demon asked:
"Hví þegir þú nú?"	"Why silent are-you now?"	"Who are you so quiet now?"
Þorsteinn anzaði, er af honum leið:.	Thorstein replied, that of him this-way:.	Thorstein replied to him this way:
"Því þegi ek, at ek undrumst, hvé mikil ógnarraust at liggr í þér, eigi meiri púki en mér sýnist þú vera, eða er þetta it mesta óp Starkaðar?".	"Because silent i-am, that i wonder, how great dreadful-voice that laid in you, no more demon than to-me seems you be, or was this the most shouting Of-Starkad".	"I am silent because I wonder, how such a dreadful voice came from you, little demon that you seem to be, and was this the loudes shouting of Starkad?"
"Eigi er nærri því", segir hann,.	"Not is near as", said he,.	"Not even close", he said,
"þetta er heldr it minnsta óp hans"..	"this is rather the quietest shouting his".	"This is rather like his quietest shrieking".
"Drag þú eigi undan lengr",	"Drag you not further long",	"Delay no further",
kvað Þorsteinn,.	said Thorstein,.	said Thorstein,
"ok lát mik heyra it mesta ópit"..	"and let me hear the most shriek".	"And let me hear the loudest shriek".

The Tale of Thorstein Shiver (Old Norse)

Old Norse	Literal	English
Púki játaði því..	The-demon agreed accordingly..	The demon agreed accordingly.
Þorsteinn bjóst þá við ok braut saman feldinn ok snaraði hann svá at höfði sér ok helt at útan báðum höndum..	Thorstein prepared then with and brought together cloak and snared it so about head his and held at of both hands..	Thorstein then prepared himself by folding the cloak, winding it around his head, and holding it with both hands.
Draugrinn hafði þokat at Þorsteini um þrjár setur við hvert ópit, ok váru þá þrjár einar á milli þeira..	The-demon had moved to Thorstein about three seats with each shriek, and was then three only in between them..	The demon had moved closer to Thorstein by three seats with each shriek, and there were only three seats between them.
Púkinn belgði þá hræðiliga hváftana ok sneri um í sér augunum ok tók at gaula svá hátt, at Þorsteini þótti ór hófi keyra, ok í því kvað við klukkan í staðnum, en Þorsteinn fell í óvit fram á gólfit..	The-demon bellowed then terribly cheeks and turned about in his eyes and took to howling so high, that Thorstein thought out-of measure exceeded, and at since cried-out with the-clock about the-place, then Thorstein fell to unconscious towards the floor..	The demon then bellowed his cheeks terribly and rolled his eyes, and began howling so loudly, that it was beyond all measure for Thorstein, and as he cried out, the church bell rang out, and Thorstein fell onconscious to the floor.
En púkanum brá svá við klukkuhljóðit, at hann steypðist niðr í gólfit, ok mátti lengi heyra yminn niðr í jörðina..	Then the-demon drew so against the-clock-sound, that he fell down to the-floor, and may long be-heard the-sound down in the-earth..	The demon reacted to the bell by tumbling to the floor, the sound could be heard for a long time down in the earth.
Þorsteinn raknaði skjótt við ok stóð upp ok gekk til sængr sinnar ok lagðist niðr..	Thorstein recovered quickly with and stood up and went to bed his and lay down..	Thorstein recovered quickly, stood up, went to his bed and lay down.

2

Old Norse	Literal	English
En er morgnaði, stóðu menn upp..	When it-was morning, stood the-men up..	When it was morning, the men stood up.
Gekk konungr til kirkju ok hlýddi tíðum..	Went the-king to church and obeyed often..	The king went to the church in his religious obedience.
Eftir þat var gengit til borða..	After that then went to the-table..	Then after that they went to the table to eat.
Konungr var ekki foraðs blíðr..	The-King was not terribly happy..	The king was not terribly happy.
Hann tók til orða:.	He took to words:.	He began to speak:

The Tale of Thorstein Shiver (Old Norse)

Old Norse	Literal	English
"Hefir nökkurr maðr farit einn saman í nátt til heimilishúss?"	"Had some man travelled alone together in the-night to-the outhouse?"	"Did somebody go alone in the night to the outhouse?"
Þorsteinn stóð þá upp ok fell fram fyrir konung ok sagðist af hafa brugðit hans boði..	Thorstein stood then up and fell forwards before the-king and said out-of had custom he asked..	Thorstein then stood up and fell before the king and said that he had disobeyed his order.
Konungr svarar:.	The-King answered:.	The king answered:
"Ekki var mér þetta svá mikil meingerð, en sýnir þú þat, sem talat er til yðvar Íslendinga, at þér séð mjök einrænir, en varð þú við nökkut varr?"	"Not was to-me this so great offence, but showed you that, which-is told that to your Icelanders, that they seem very-much stubborn, but were you with something aware?"	"It was not so great an offence to me, but it shows what is said about you Icelanders, that you are very stubborn, but were you aware of something?"
Þorsteinn sagði þá alla sögu, sem farit hafði..	Thorstein said then all said, as went had..	Thorstein then told him all that had happened.
Konungr spurði:.	The-King asked:.	The king asked:
"Hví þótti þér gagn, at hann æpði?".	"Why seemed to-you benefit, that he shrieked".	"What benefit did you seek from his shrieking?"
"Þat vil ek segja yðr, herra..	"That will i say to-you, lord..	"I will tell you, lord.
Ek þóttist þat vita, með því at þér höfðuð varat alla menn við at fara þangat einir saman, en skelmirinn kom upp, at vit mundim eigi klaklaust skilja, en ek ætlaða, at þér mundið vakna við, herra, er hann æpði, ok þóttumst ek þá hólpinn, ef þér yrðið varir við"..	I thought that certainly, with since that you had warned all men against to go there alone together, when the-demon came up, then knew would not unhurt know, but i supposed, that you would awake with, lord, when he shrieked, and thought i then to-be-helped, if you had-been aware with".	I thought that it was certain, that since you warned everyone against going alone, when the demon appeared, then he would not leave the place unharmed, but I supposed that if you were to wake up, lord, when he shrieked, that I might be helped, if you had been aware of it".
"Svá var ok",	"So was and",	"So it was, and...",
sagði konungr,.	said the-king,.	said the king,
"at ek vaknaða við, ok svá vissa ek, hvat fram fór, ok því lét ek hringja, at ek vissa, at eigi mundi þér ella duga..	"that i woke-up with, and so knew i, what from-going forwards, and accordingly had i rung, that i knew, that not would you otherwise be-helped..	"...at this I woke up, and I knew what was happening, and accordingly I had the church bells rung, as I knew, that nothing else could help you.

The Tale of Thorstein Shiver (Old Norse)

Old Norse	Literal	English
En hræddist þú ekki, þá er púkinn tók at æpa?"	But frightened you not, then when the-demon took to shrieking?"	But were you not frightened then, when you heard the demon shrieking?"
Þorsteinn svarar:.	Thorstein answered:.	Thorstein answered:
"Ek veit ekki, hvat þat er, hræðslan, herra"..	"I know not, how to be, afraid, lord".	"I do not know how to be afraid, lord".
"Var engi ótti í brjósti þér?"	"Was no fear in breast yours?"	"Was there no fear in your breast?",
sagði konungr..	said the-king..	said the king.
"Eigi var þat",	"None was that",	"That was not so...",
sagði Þorsteinn,.	said Thorstein,.	said Thorstein,
"því at við it síðasta ópit skaut mér næsta skelk í bringu"..	"then that with the last shriek shot me next-to shivered in chest".	"...because with that last shriek, I nearly shivered in my chest".
Konungr svarar:.	The-King answered:.	The-king answered:
"Nú skal auka nafn þitt ok kalla þik Þorstein skelk heðan af, ok er hér sverð, at ek vil gefa þér at nafnfesti"..	"Now shall extra name yours and call you Thorstein shiver from-here of, and is here a-sword, that i wish to-give to-you as a-nickname".	"Now I shall add an extra name to yours and call you Thorstein Shiver from now on, and here is a sword, that I wish to give you for your nickname".
Þorsteinn þakkaði honum..	Thorstein thanked him..	Thorstein thanked him.
Svá er sagt, at Þorsteinn gerðist hirðmaðr Óláfs konungs ok var með honum síðan ok fell á Orminum langa með öðrum köppum konungs..	So was said, that Thorstein became court-man Olaf's the-king and was with him since and fell on The-serpent long with other champions the-king's..	And so it was said, that Thorstein became a court man of King Olaf and was with him ever since, until he fell on Olaf's longship 'The Serpent' alongside the king's other champions.

Word List (Old Norse to English)

Word List (Old Norse to English)

Old Norse	English

A, a

af	from, of, of, out-of
aldri	never
alla	all, all
allt	all
annan	second
annars	other
annat	else
anzaði	replied
at	about, as, at, from, that, then, to
auðunarsonar	son-of-Audun (name)
augunum	eyes
auka	extra
austr	east

Á, á

á	about, all, from, in, of, on, so, that, the, was, with
áðr	before
ásgeirssonar	son-of-Asgeir (name)

Æ, æ

æðikolls	rage-head
æp	shriek
æpa	shrieking
æpði	shrieked
æpir	cries-out
ætlaða	supposed

B, b

báðum	both
bæ	a-farm
beiddi	needed
beiddist	ask
belgði	bellowed

Old Norse	English
betr	better
bezt	best
bjóst	prepared
blíðr	happy
boði	asked
borða	the-table
brá	drew
braut	brought
brennanda	burning
bringu	chest
brjósti	breast
brugðit	custom

D, d

dólgrinn	the-demon
drag	drag
draugr	the-demon
draugrinn	the-demon
drekka	drank
drykkjuborð	drinking-tables
drykkjuborðum	drinking-tables
drýsildjöflanna	petty-devils
duga	be-helped

E, e

eða	but, or
ef	if
eftir	after, following
eigi	no, none, not, not-to
einar	only
einir	alone
einn	a, alone
einrænir	stubborn
ek	I, I-am
ekki	not
eldinum	the-flames
ella	or-else, otherwise
ellifu	eleven
en	and, but, than, then, when

Word List (Old Norse to English)

Old Norse	English
engi	no, none
er	as, be, is, it-was, that, was, were, when, which, who, who-was

F, f

Old Norse	English
fætr	feet
fáfnisbani	Fafnisbani (name)
fara	go
farit	travelled, went
fast	fast
feld	cloak
feldarskautinu	fur-cloak
feldinn	cloak
feldinum	cloak
fell	fell
ferr	away
firn	monstrous
fjandi	a-fiend
fjarri	far
fjölmennr	followers
fjöndunum	the-torment
flest	most
fór	forwards, went
foraðs	terribly
fram	forwards, from-going, towards
fyrir	before, for
fyrr	before

G, g

Old Norse	English
gagn	benefit
gamli	old
ganga	go
gat	could
gaul	a-howl
gaula	howling
gaulat	bellow
gefa	to-give
gekk	went
gengit	went
gengr	went
gengu	went
gerðist	became
gerir	did
gólfit	floor, the-floor

H, h

Old Norse	English
hafa	had, have
hafði	had
hann	he, him, it
hans	he, his
haraldi	Harald (name)
hátt	high
heðan	from-here
hefir	had, has, has-been
heimilishúss	outhouse, the-outhouse
heitir	named
heldr	rather
helt	held
helvíti	hell
hér	here
herra	lord
hét	named
heyra	be-heard, hear
hilditönn	war-tooth
hinn	he
hirðmaðr	court-man
hjá	beside
hlýða	obey
hlýddi	obeyed
höfði	head
höfðuð	had
hófi	measure
hólpinn	to-be-helped
höndum	hands
honum	he, him
hræ	corpses
hræddist	frightened
hræðiliga	terribly
hræðslan	afraid
hraustr	brave
hringja	rung
hús	house
hvaðan	from-where

Word List (Old Norse to English)

Old Norse	English
hváftana	cheeks
hváftunum	cheeks
hvárum	each
hvat	how, what
hvé	how
hverir	who
hverja	what
hverr	each, who
hvers	what
hversu	how-so
hvert	each
hví	why

I, i

iljarnar	soles-of-the-feet
illa	badly
inn	the
innstu	the-innermost
it	the

Í, í

í	a, about, at, in, of, to
íslendinga	Icelanders
íslendingr	the-Icelander
íslenzkr	Icelandic

J, j

jafnlítill	as-small
játaði	agreed
jörðina	the-earth

K, k

kalla	call
kanntu	can-you
kappa	hero
kemr	came
keyra	exceeded
kippir	drew

Old Norse	English
kirkju	church
klaklaust	unhurt
klukkan	the-clock
klukkuhljóðit	the-clock-sound
kom	came
kominn	come
komit	come
konung	the-king
konungi	the-king
konungr	the-king
konungs	the-king, the-king's
köppum	champions
kvað	asked, be-called, cried-out, said
kveldit	evening, the-evening
kyndarinn	the-kindling
kyndir	kindles

L, l

lá	lay
lagðist	lay
langa	long
lát	let
leið	during, this-way
lengi	long
lengr	long
lét	had
liggr	laid
litit	considered
lítt	a-little

M, m

má	may
maðr	a-man, man
mælti	spoke
mátti	may
máttu	might
með	with
megin	may
megum	may
meingerð	offence
meiri	more

Word List (Old Norse to English)

Old Norse	English
menn	men, the-men
mér	me, to-me
mest	mostly
mesta	most
mik	me
mikil	great, much
mikit	great, much
milli	between
minnsta	quietest
mjök	many, much, very-much
mönnum	men
morgnaði	morning
mundi	would
mundið	would
mundim	would
mundu	will

N, n

Old Norse	English
náðir	mercy
nærri	near
næsta	next-to
nafn	name
nafnfesti	a-nickname
nátt	the-night
náttina	night-time, the-night
niðr	down
nökkura	some
nökkurr	some
nökkut	somehow, something
nú	now
nýkominn	newly-come

O, o

Old Norse	English
ofan	downed
ofn	the-oven
ok	and
orða	words
orminum	the-serpent
oss	to-us

Ó, ó

Old Norse	English
ógnarraust	dreadful-voice
óláfr	Olaf (name)
óláfs	Olaf's (name)
ómegin	un-mighty
óp	cries-out, shouting
ópi	shrieking
ópit	open, shriek
ór	from, out-of
ósvipt	un-thrown
ótti	fear
óvit	unconscious

Ö, ö

Old Norse	English
öðrum	other
öklaeld	ankle-fire
öskurliga	terribly

P, p

Old Norse	English
pína	torment
pínu	torment
písl	torment
píslir	the-torment, torment
púkanum	the-demon
púki	a-demon, demon, the-demon
púkinn	the-demon

R, r

Old Norse	English
raknaði	recovered
reinu	Reim (place)
rekkjufélaga	bed-fellow
rétt	right

S, s

Old Norse	English
sá	so
sæng	the-bed

Word List (Old Norse to English)

Old Norse	English
sængr	bed
sagði	said
sagðist	said
sagðr	said
sagt	said
salerni	toilet
saman	together
sat	sat
sátu	sitting
séð	seem
segir	said
segja	say
sem	as, which-is, who
sér	his, saw, them
setit	sat
setti	put
setu	seat
setur	seats
sezt	sat
síðan	since
síðasta	last
sigurðr	Sigurd (name)
sik	himself
sín	himself
sinn	their
sinnar	his
sitja	sit
sjá	such
sjálfr	himself
skal	shall
skaut	shot
skelk	shiver, shivered
skelmirinn	the-demon
skilja	know
skjótt	quickly
skökuls	shaft
skóm	his-shoes
skyldi	should
slíkum	such
sló	struck
snaraði	snared
sneri	turned
sofa	sleep
sögu	said
spurði	asked
spyrja	ask
staðar	places
staðnum	the-place
standa	stand
starkaðar	of-Starkad (name)
starkaði	Starkad (name)
starkaðr	Starkad (name)
stendr	stood
steypðist	fell
stóð	stood
stóðu	stood
stórt	a-large
stund	while
sumarit	summer
sundr	down
svá	so
svaf	slept
svarar	answered
sverð	a-sword
sýnir	showed
sýnist	seems

T, t

Old Norse	English
talaði	told
talat	told
tekr	took
tíðum	often
til	to, to-the
tíma	time
tók	took

Þ, þ

Old Norse	English
þá	that, then, there
þaðan	of-there
þakkaði	thanked
þangat	there
þar	that, there
þat	it, that, to
þegi	silent
þegir	silent
þeim	them
þeira	them

Word List (Old Norse to English)

Old Norse	English
þér	they, to-you, you, yours
þess	this
þetta	this
þik	you
þitt	yours
þó	then, though
þokat	moved
þola	endures
þolir	endures
þorkell	Thorkel (name)
þorkelsson	son-of-Thorkel (name)
þorstein	Thorstein (name)
þorsteini	Thorstein (name)
þorsteinn	Thorstein (name)
þorsteirm	Thorstein (name)
þótti	seemed, thought
þóttist	thought
þóttumst	thought
þrjár	three
þú	are-you, you
þunni	thin
því	accordingly, as, because, since, then, therefore
þykkir	seems
þykkvan	thick

U, u

um	about, around
undan	further
undrumst	wonder
upp	above, up

Ú, ú

útan	of

V, v

vafði	wrapped
vakna	awake
vaknaða	woke-up
vaknaði	awoke
var	then, was, was-with
varat	warned
varð	was, were
varir	aware
varr	aware
várt	us
váru	was, were
veit	know
veizlu	a-feast
veizlum	feasts
vekja	awake
vel	well
vér	we
vera	be
verit	been
verst	the-worst
vetrinn	winter
við	against, with
víðara	wider
víkina	Vik (place)
vil	will, wish
vildi	willed
villtu	will-you
vissa	knew
vissi	knew
víst	certainly
vit	knew
vita	certainly

Y, y

yðr	to-you
yðvar	your
yfir	about, over
yminn	the-sound
yrðið	had-been
yztu	the-outermost

Word List (English to Old Norse)

Word List (English to Old Norse)

English	Old Norse

A, a

English	Old Norse
a	einn, í
about	á, at, í, um, yfir
above	upp
accordingly	því
a-demon	púki
a-farm	bæ
a-feast	veizlu
a-fiend	fjandi
afraid	hræðslan
after	eftir
against	við
agreed	játaði
a-howl	gaul
a-large	stórt
a-little	lítt
all	á, alla, alla, allt
alone	einir, einn
a-man	maðr
and	en, ok
a-nickname	nafnfesti
ankle-fire	öklaeld
answered	svarar
are-you	þú
around	um
as	at, er, sem, því
ask	beiddist, spyrja
asked	boði, kvað, spurði
as-small	jafnlítill
a-sword	sverð
at	at, í
awake	vakna, vekja
aware	varir, varr
away	ferr
awoke	vaknaði

B, b

English	Old Norse
badly	illa
be	er, vera
be-called	kvað
became	gerðist
because	því
bed	sængr
bed-fellow	rekkjufélaga
been	verit
before	áðr, fyrir, fyrr
be-heard	heyra
be-helped	duga
bellow	gaulat
bellowed	belgði
benefit	gagn
beside	hjá
best	bezt
better	betr
between	milli
both	báðum
brave	hraustr
breast	brjósti
brought	braut
burning	brennanda
but	eða, en

C, c

English	Old Norse
call	kalla
came	kemr, kom
can-you	kanntu
certainly	víst, vita
champions	köppum
cheeks	hváftana, hváftunum
chest	bringu
church	kirkju
cloak	feld, feldinn, feldinum
come	kominn, komit
considered	litit
corpses	hræ
could	gat
court-man	hirðmaðr
cried-out	kvað
cries-out	æpir, óp
custom	brugðit

Word List (English to Old Norse)

English	Old Norse	English	Old Norse
		from-here	heðan
		from-where	hvaðan
		fur-cloak	feldarskautinu
		further	undan

D, d

English	Old Norse
demon	púki
did	gerir
down	niðr, sundr
downed	ofan
drag	drag
drank	drekka
dreadful-voice	ógnarraust
drew	brá, kippir
drinking-tables	drykkjuborð, drykkjuborðum
during	leið

E, e

English	Old Norse
each	hvárum, hverr, hvert
east	austr
eleven	ellifu
else	annat
endures	þola, þolir
evening	kveldit
exceeded	keyra
extra	auka
eyes	augunum

F, f

English	Old Norse
Fafnisbani (name)	fáfnisbani
far	fjarri
fast	fast
fear	ótti
feasts	veizlum
feet	fætr
fell	fell, steypðist
floor	gólfit
followers	fjölmennr
following	eftir
for	fyrir
forwards	fór, fram
frightened	hræddist
from	á, af, at, ór
from-going	fram

G, g

English	Old Norse
go	fara, ganga
great	mikil, mikit

H, h

English	Old Norse
had	hafa, hafði, hefir, höfðuð, lét
had-been	yrðið
hands	höndum
happy	blíðr
Harald (name)	haraldi
has	hefir
has-been	hefir
have	hafa
he	hann, hans, hinn, honum
head	höfði
hear	heyra
held	helt
hell	helvíti
here	hér
hero	kappa
high	hátt
him	hann, honum
himself	sik, sín, sjálfr
his	hans, sér, sinnar
his-shoes	skóm
house	hús
how	hvat, hvé
howling	gaula
how-so	hversu

I, i

English	Old Norse
I	ek
I-am	ek

Word List (English to Old Norse)

English	Old Norse
Icelanders	íslendinga
Icelandic	íslenzkr
if	ef
in	á, í
is	er
it	hann, þat
it-was	er

K, k

kindles	kyndir
knew	vissa, vissi, vit
know	skilja, veit

L, l

laid	liggr
last	síðasta
lay	lá, lagðist
let	lát
long	langa, lengi, lengr
lord	herra

M, m

man	maðr
many	mjök
may	má, mátti, megin, megum
me	mér, mik
measure	hófi
men	menn, mönnum
mercy	náðir
might	máttu
monstrous	firn
more	meiri
morning	morgnaði
most	flest, mesta
mostly	mest
moved	þokat
much	mikil, mikit, mjök

N, n

name	nafn
named	heitir, hét
near	nærri
needed	beiddi
never	aldri
newly-come	nýkominn
next-to	næsta
night-time	náttina
no	eigi, engi
none	eigi, engi
not	eigi, ekki
not-to	eigi
now	nú

O, o

obey	hlýða
obeyed	hlýddi
of	á, af, af, í, útan
offence	meingerð
of-Starkad (name)	starkaðar
often	tíðum
of-there	þaðan
Olaf (name)	óláfr
Olaf's (name)	óláfs
old	gamli
on	á
only	einar
open	ópit
or	eða
or-else	ella
other	annars, öðrum
otherwise	ella
outhouse	heimilishúss
out-of	af, ór
over	yfir

P, p

petty-devils	drýsildjöflanna
places	staðar

Word List (English to Old Norse)

English	Old Norse	English	Old Norse
prepared	bjóst	Sigurd (name)	sigurðr
put	setti	silent	þegi, þegir
		since	síðan, því
		sit	sitja
		sitting	sátu
		sleep	sofa
		slept	svaf
		snared	snaraði
		so	á, sá, svá
		soles-of-the-feet	iljarnar
		some	nökkura, nökkurr
		somehow	nökkut
		something	nökkut
		son-of-Asgeir (name)	ásgeirssonar
		son-of-Audun (name)	auðunarsonar
		son-of-Thorkel (name)	þorkelsson
		spoke	mælti
		stand	standa
		Starkad (name)	starkaði, starkaðr
		stood	stendr, stóð, stóðu
		struck	sló
		stubborn	einrænir
		such	sjá, slíkum
		summer	sumarit
		supposed	ætlaða

Q, q

English	Old Norse
quickly	skjótt
quietest	minnsta

R, r

English	Old Norse
rage-head	æðikolls
rather	heldr
recovered	raknaði
Reim (place)	reinu
replied	anzaði
right	rétt
rung	hringja

S, s

English	Old Norse
said	kvað, sagði, sagðist, sagðr, sagt, segir, sögu
sat	sat, setit, sezt
saw	sér
say	segja
seat	setu
seats	setur
second	annan
seem	séð
seemed	þótti
seems	sýnist, þykkir
shaft	skökuls
shall	skal
shiver	skelk
shivered	skelk
shot	skaut
should	skyldi
shouting	óp
showed	sýnir
shriek	æp, ópit
shrieked	æpði
shrieking	æpa, ópi

T, t

English	Old Norse
terribly	foraðs, hræðiliga, öskurliga
than	en
thanked	þakkaði
that	á, at, er, þá, þar, þat
the	á, inn, it
the-bed	sæng
the-clock	klukkan
the-clock-sound	klukkuhljóðit
the-demon	dólgrinn, draugr, draugrinn, púkanum, púki, púkinn, skelmirinn
the-earth	jörðina
the-evening	kveldit
the-flames	eldinum

Word List (English to Old Norse)

English	Old Norse	*English*	Old Norse
the-floor	gólfit	*towards*	fram
the-Icelander	íslendingr	*to-you*	þér, yðr
the-innermost	innstu	*travelled*	farit
their	sinn	*turned*	sneri
the-kindling	kyndarinn		
the-king	konung, konungi, konungr, konungs		

U, u

English	Old Norse
the-king's	konungs
them	sér, þeim, þeira
the-men	menn
then	at, en, þá, þó, því, var
the-night	nátt, náttina
the-outermost	yztu
the-outhouse	heimilishúss
the-oven	ofn
the-place	staðnum

English	Old Norse
unconscious	óvit
unhurt	klaklaust
un-mighty	ómegin
un-thrown	ósvipt
up	upp
us	várt

V, v

there	þá, þangat, þar
therefore	því
the-serpent	orminum
the-sound	yminn
the-table	borða
the-torment	fjöndunum, píslir
the-worst	verst
they	þér
thick	þykkvan
thin	þunni

English	Old Norse
very-much	mjök
Vik (place)	víkina

W, w

this	þess, þetta
this-way	leið
Thorkel (name)	þorkell
Thorstein (name)	þorstein, þorsteini, þorsteinn, þorsteirm

English	Old Norse
warned	varat
war-tooth	hilditönn
was	á, er, var, varð, váru
was-with	var
we	vér
well	vel
went	farit, fór, gekk, gengit, gengr, gengu
were	er, varð, váru
what	hvat, hverja, hvers
when	en, er
which	er
which-is	sem
while	stund
who	er, hverir, hverr, sem
who-was	er
why	hví
wider	víðara
will	mundu, vil
willed	vildi
will-you	villtu
winter	vetrinn

though	þó
thought	þótti, þóttist, þóttumst
three	þrjár
time	tíma
to	at, í, þat, til
to-be-helped	hólpinn
together	saman
to-give	gefa
toilet	salerni
told	talaði, talat
to-me	mér
took	tekr, tók
torment	pína, pínu, písl, píslir
to-the	til
to-us	oss

Word List (English to Old Norse)

English	Old Norse
wish	vil
with	á, með, við
woke-up	vaknaða
wonder	undrumst
words	orða
would	mundi, mundið, mundim
wrapped	vafði

Y, y

you	þér, þik, þú
your	yðvar
yours	þér, þitt

The Tale of Thorstein Shiver (*Old Icelandic*)

Old Icelandic	Literal	English
1	**1**	**1**
Það er sagt um sumarið eftir að Ólafur konungur fór að veislum austur um Víkina og víðara annarstaðar.	It is said about summer following that Olaf the-king went to feasts east around Vik and wider other-places.	It is said that the following summer, King Olaf went to feasts in the east around Vik and wider to other places.
Tók hann veislu á þeim bæ er á Reimi heitir.	Took he a-feast with them a-farm which was Reim named.	He took a feast at a farm called Reim.
Hann var mjög fjölmennur.	He was-with many followers.	He was with many followers.
Sá var maður þá með konungi er Þorsteinn hét Þorkelsson, Ásgeirssonar æðikolls, Auðunarsonar skökuls, íslenskur maður, og hafði komið til konungs um veturinn áður.	So was a-man there with the-king who-was Thorstein named Son-of-Thorkel, Son-of-Asgeir rage-head, Son-of-Audun shaft, Icelandic man, and had come to the-king's about winter before.	Also there with the king was a man named Thorstein, the son of Thorkel, the son of Asgeir Rage-Head, son of Audun Shaft, an Icelander man, and he had come to the king around the winter before.
Um kveldið er menn sátu yfir drykkjuborðum talaði Ólafur konungur að engi maður af hans mönnum skyldi einn saman fara í salerni um náttina því að hver sem ganga beiddist skyldi með sér kalla sinn rekkjufélaga ella kvað hann eigi mundu hlýða.	About evening were the-men sitting over drinking-tables told Olaf the-king that no man of his men should alone together go to toilet about night-time therefore that each who go ask should with them call their bed-fellow or-else be-called him not will obey.	About evening, the men were sitting at the drinking tables, and Olaf the king made a speech, that none of his men should go alone to the toilet during the night, and that anyone who must go, should ask their bed fellow to accompany them, or they will have disobeyed him.
Drekka menn nú vel um kveldið en er ofan voru drykkjuborð gengu menn að sofa.	Drank the-men now well about the-evening and when downed were drinking-tables went men to sleep.	The men now drank well into the evening, and when the drinking tables were taken down, the men went to sleep.
Og er á leið náttina vaknaði Þorsteinn Íslendingur og beiddi að ganga af sæng en sá svaf fast er hjá honum lá svo að Þorsteinn vildi víst eigi vekja hann.	And when that during the-night awoke Thorstein The-Icelander and needed to go from the-bed but so slept fast was beside him lay so that Thorstein willed certainly not-to awake him.	And during the night, Thorstein the Icelander awoke and needed to go from his bed, but he who was beside him was fast asleep, so that Thorstein did not want to wake him.

The Tale of Thorstein Shiver (Old Icelandic)

Old Icelandic	Literal	English
Stendur hann þá upp og kippir skóm á fætur sér og tekur yfir sig einn feld þykkvan og gengur til heimilishúss.	Stood he then up and drew his-shoes about feet his and took about himself a cloak thick and went to the-outhouse.	He then stood up, put his shoes on his feet, and drew a thick cloak around him, and went to the outhouse.
Það var stórt hús svo að ellefu menn máttu sitja hvoru megin.	It was a-large house so that eleven men might sit each may.	It was a large outhouse, that might have fit eleven men sitting.
Sest hann á ystu setu.	Sat he on the-outermost seat.	He sat on the outermost seat,
Og er hann hefir setið nokkura stund sér hann að púki kemur upp á innstu setu og sat þar.	And as he had sat some while saw he that a-demon came up from the-innermost seat and sat there.	and as he sat there for a while, he saw that a demon came up from the innermost seat and sat there.
Þorsteinn mælti þá:	Thorstein spoke then:	Then Thorstein spoke:
"Hver er þar kominn?"	"Who is that come?"	"Who is that there?"
Dólgurinn svarar:	The-demon answered:	The-demon answered:
"Hér er kominn Þorkell hinn þunni er féll á hræ með Haraldi konungi hilditönn".	"Here is come Thorkel the thin who fell about corpses with Harald the-king war-tooth".	"Here is Thorkel the Thin, who fell about corpses with king Harald Wartooth".
"Hvaðan komst þú nú að?"	"From-where came you now to?"	"Where did you come from?"
kvað Þorsteinn.	said Thorstein.	said Thorstein.
Hann sagðist nú nýkominn að úr helvíti.	He said now newly-come from out-of hell.	He said that he had newly come from hell.
"Hvað kanntu þaðan að segja?"	"What can-you of-there to say?"	"What can you tell me me about it there?"
spurði Þorsteinn.	asked Thorstein.	asked Thorstein.
Hinn svarar:	He answered:	He answered:
"Hvers viltu spyrja?"	"What will-you ask?"	"What do you want to know?"
"Hverjir þola best píslir í helvíti?"	"Who endures best the-torment in hell?"	"Who endures the torments of hell best?"
"Engi betur",	"None better".	"There is none better...",

The Tale of Thorstein Shiver (Old Icelandic)

Old Icelandic	Literal	English
kvað púki,	said the-demon,	said the demon,
"en Sigurður Fáfnisbani".	"than Sigurd Fafnisbani".	"...than Sigurd Fafnisbani".
"Hverja písl hefir hann?"	"What torment has he?"	"What torment does he have?"
"Hann kyndir ofn brennanda",	"He kindles the-oven burning".	"He kindles the oven burning",
sagði draugurinn.	said the-demon.	said the demon.
"Ekki þykir mér það svo mikil písl",	"Not seems to-me that so much torment".	"That does not seem to me to be such a torment",
segir Þorsteinn.	said Thorstein.	said Thorstein.
"Eigi er það þó",	"Not is that though".	"It's not that though",
kvað púki,	said the-demon,	said the demon,
"því að hann er sjálfur kyndarinn".	"because that he is himself the-kindling".	"Because he himself is the kindling".
"Mikið er það þá",	"Much is that then".	"That is very much then",
kvað Þorsteinn,	said Thorstein,	said Thorstein.
"eða hver þolir þar verst píslir?"	"but who endures there the-worst torment?"	"But who endures the worst torment?"
Draugurinn svarar:	The-demon answered:	The demon answered:
"Starkaður hinn gamli þolir verst því að hann æpir svo að oss fjandunum er það meiri pína en flest allt annað svo að vér megum fyrir hans ópi aldrei náðir hafa".	"Starkad the old endures the-worst, because that he cries-out so, that to-us the-torment is that more torment than most all else, so that we may for his shrieking never mercy have".	"Starkad the Old endures it worst, because he cries out so much, that to us the torment is worse than anything else, so that we may have mercy from his shrieking".
"Hvað pínu hefir hann þess",	"What torment has he this".	"What torment does he have?...",
kvað Þorsteinn,	said Thorstein,	said Thorstein,
"er hann þolir svo illa, svo hraustur maður sem hann hefir sagður verið?"	"that he endures so badly, so brave a-man as he has-been said been?"	"...that he endures it so badly, such a brave man as has been said to be?"

The Tale of Thorstein Shiver (Old Icelandic)

Old Icelandic	Literal	English
"Hann hefir ökklaeld".	"He has ankle-fire".	"He has fire up to his ankles".
"Ekki þykir mér það svo mikið",	"Not seems to-me that so much".	"That does not seem to me to be so much...",
sagði Þorsteinn,	said Thorstein,	said Thorstein,
"slíkum kappa sem hann hefir verið".	"such hero as he has been".	"...such a hero as he has been".
"Ekki er þá rétt á litið",	"Not is that right all considered".	"Then you have not considered it all correctly...",
kvað draugur,	said the-demon,	said the demon,
"því að iljarnar einar standa upp úr eldinum".	"because that soles-of-the-feet only stand above from the-flames".	"...because only the soles of his feet are sticking out from the flames".
"Mikið er það",	"Much is that".	"That is a lot then",
kvað Þorsteinn,	said Thorstein,	said Thorstein,
"og æp þú eftir honum nokkuð óp".	"and shriek you after him somehow cries-out".	"And now, shriek something like how he does, once".
"Það skal vera",	"That shall be".	"So it shall be",
kvað púki.	said the-demon.	said the demon.
Hann sló þá í sundur á sér hvoftunum og setti upp gaul mikið en Þorsteinn brá feldarskautinu að höfði sér.	He struck then to down of his cheeks and put up a-howl great but Thorstein drew fur-cloak about head his.	He then threw open his jaws and put up a great howl, but Thorstein drew his fur cloak about his head.
Honum varð mjög ósvipt við óp þetta og mælti:	He was much un-thrown with shouting this and spoke:	He remained unmoved at this shouting and spoke:
"Æpir hann þetta ópið mest svo?"	"Cries-out he this open mostly so?"	"Is that the most he cries out?"
"Fjarri fer um það",	"Far away about that".	"Far from it...",
kvað draugur,	said the-demon,	said the demon,
"því að þetta er óp vort drýsildjöflanna".	"because that this is shouting us petty-devils".	"...because that is the shouting of us petty devils".

The Tale of Thorstein Shiver (Old Icelandic)

Old Icelandic	Literal	English
"Æp þú eftir Starkaði líttað", kvað Þorsteinn.	"Shriek you after Starkad a-little". asked Thorstein.	"Shriek like Starkad does a little then", asked Thorstein.
"Það má vel",	"That may well".	"So it shall be",
kvað púki.	said the-demon.	said the demon.
Tekur hann þá að æpa í annan tíma svo öskurlega að Þorsteini þótti firn í hversu mikið sjá fjandi jafnlítill gat gaulað.	Took he then to shrieking a second time so terribly that Thorstein thought monstrous of how-so great such a-fiend as-small could bellow.	He took to sheirking a second time so terribly, that Thorstein thought it was monstrous, that such a little fiend could bellow so loudly.
Þorsteinn gerir þá sem fyrr að hann vafði feldinum að höfði sér og brá honum þó svo við að ómegin var á honum svo að hann vissi ekki til sín.	Thorstein did then as before that he wrapped cloak about head his and drew he then so against that un-mighty was so he so that he knew not to himself.	Thorstein then did as before, and wrapped his cloak around his head, but the shrieking paralysed him, and he fainted.
Þá spurði púkinn:	Then asked the-demon:	Then the demon asked:
"Hví þegir þú nú?"	"Why silent are-you now?"	"Who are you so quiet now?"
Þorsteinn ansaði er af honum leið:	Thorstein replied that of him this-way:	Thorstein replied to him this way:
"Því þegi eg að eg undrast hve mikil ógnarraust að liggur í þér, eigi meiri púki en mér sýnist þú vera eða er þetta hið mesta óp Starkaðar?"	"Because silent i-am that i wonder how great dreadful-voice that laid in you, no more demon than to-me seems you be or was this the most shouting Of-Starkad?"	"I am silent because I wonder, how such a dreadful voice came from you, little demon that you seem to be, and was this the loudes shouting of Starkad?"
"Eigi er nærri því.	"Not is near as.	"Not even close.
Þetta er",	This is",	This is",
segir hann, "heldur hið minnsta óp hans".	said he, "rather the quietest shouting his".	he said, "rather like his quietest shrieking".
"Drag þú eigi undan lengur",	"Drag you not further long".	"Delay no further",
kvað Þorsteinn,	said Thorstein,	said Thorstein,
"og lát mig heyra hið mesta ópið".	"and let me hear the most shriek".	"And let me hear the loudest shriek".

The Tale of Thorstein Shiver (Old Icelandic)

Old Icelandic	Literal	English
Púki játtaði því.	The-demon agreed accordingly.	The demon agreed accordingly.
Þorsteinn bjóst þá við og braut saman feldinn og snaraði hann svo að höfði sér og hélt að utan báðum höndum.	Thorstein prepared then with and brought together cloak and snared it so about head his and held at of both hands.	Thorstein then prepared himself by folding the cloak, winding it around his head, and holding it with both hands.
Draugurinn hafði þokað að Þorsteini um þrjár setur við hvert ópið og voru þá þrjár einar á milli þeirra.	The-demon had moved to Thorstein about three seats with each shriek and was then three only in between them.	The demon had moved closer to Thorstein by three seats with each shriek, and there were only three seats between them.
Púkinn belgdi þá hræðilega hvoftana og sneri um í sér augunum og tók að gaula svo hátt að Þorsteini þótti úr hófi keyra og í því kvað við klukkan í staðnum en Þorsteinn féll í óvit fram á gólfið.	The-demon bellowed then terribly cheeks and turned about in his eyes and took to howling so high that Thorstein thought out-of measure exceeded and at since cried-out with the-clock about the-place then Thorstein fell to unconscious towards the floor.	The demon then bellowed his cheeks terribly and rolled his eyes, and began howling so loudly, that it was beyond all measure for Thorstein, and as he cried out, the church bell rang out, and Thorstein fell onconscious to the floor.
En púkanum brá svo við klukkuhljóðið að hann steyptist niður í gólfið og mátti lengi heyra yminn niður í jörðina.	Then the-demon drew so against the-clock-sound that he fell down to the-floor and may long be-heard the-sound down in the-earth.	The demon reacted to the bell by tumbling to the floor, the sound could be heard for a long time down in the earth.
Þorsteinn raknaði skjótt við og stóð upp og gekk til sængur sinnar og lagðist niður.	Thorstein recovered quickly with and stood up and went to bed his and lay down.	Thorstein recovered quickly, stood up, went to his bed and lay down.

2

En er morgnaði stóðu menn upp.	When it-was morning stood the-men up.	When it was morning, the men stood up.
Gekk konungur til kirkju og hlýddi tíðum.	Went the-king to church and obeyed often.	The king went to the church in his religious obedience.
Eftir það var gengið til borða.	After that then went to the-table.	Then after that they went to the table to eat.
Konungur var ekki forað blíður.	The-King was not terribly happy.	The king was not terribly happy.
Hann tók til orða:	He took to words:	He began to speak:

The Tale of Thorstein Shiver (Old Icelandic)

Old Icelandic	Literal	English
"Hefir nokkur maður farið einn saman í nátt til heimilishúss?"	"Had some man travelled alone together in the-night to-the outhouse?"	"Did somebody go alone in the night to the outhouse?"
Þorsteinn stóð þá upp og féll fram fyrir konung og sagðist af hafa brugðið hans boði.	Thorstein stood then up and fell forwards before the-king and said out-of had custom he asked.	Thorstein then stood up and fell before the king and said that he had disobeyed his order.
Konungur svarar:	The-King answered:	The king answered:
"Ekki var mér þetta svo mikil meingerð, en sýnir þú það sem talað er til yðvar Íslendinga að þér séuð mjög einrænir en varðst þú við nokkuð var?"	"Not was to-me this so great offence, but showed you that which-is told that to your Icelanders that they seem very-much stubborn but were you with something aware?"	"It was not so great an offence to me, but it shows what is said about you Icelanders, that you are very stubborn, but were you aware of something?"
Þorsteinn sagði þá alla sögu sem farið hafði.	Thorstein said then all said as went had.	Thorstein then told him all that had happened.
Konungur spurði:	The-King asked:	The king asked:
"Hví þótti þér gagn að hann æpti?"	"Why seemed to-you benefit that he shrieked?"	"What benefit did you seek from his shrieking?"
"Það vil eg segja yður herra.	"That will i say to-you lord.	"I will tell you, lord.
Eg þóttist það vita með því að þér höfðuð varað alla menn við að fara þangað einir saman, en skelmirinn kom upp, að við mundum eigi klakklaust skilja en eg ætlaði að þér munduð vakna við herra er hann æpti og þóttist eg þá hólpinn ef þér yrðuð varir við".	I thought that certainly with since that you had warned all men against to go there alone together, when the-demon came up, then knew would not unhurt know but i supposed that you would awake with lord when he shrieked and thought i then to-be-helped if you had-been aware with".	I thought that it was certain, that since you warned everyone against going alone, when the demon appeared, then he would not leave the place unharmed, but I supposed that if you were to wake up, lord, when he shrieked, that I might be helped, if you had been aware of it".
"Svo var og",	"So was and".	"So it was, and...",
sagði konungur,	said the-king,	said the king,
"að eg vaknaði við og svo vissi eg hvað fram fór og því lét eg hringja að eg vissi að eigi mundi þér ella duga.	"that i woke-up with and so knew i what from-going forwards and accordingly had i rung that i knew that not would you otherwise be-helped.	"...at this I woke up, and I knew what was happening, and accordingly I had the church bells rung, as I knew, that nothing else could help you.

The Tale of Thorstein Shiver (Old Icelandic)

Old Icelandic	Literal	English
En hræddist þú ekki þá er púkinn tók að æpa?"	But frightened you not then when the-demon took to shrieking?"	But were you not frightened then, when you heard the demon shrieking?"
Þorsteinn svarar:	Thorstein answered:	Thorstein answered:
"Eg veit ekki hvað það er, hræðslan, herra".	"I know not how to be, afraid, lord".	"I do not know how to be afraid, lord".
"Var engi ótti í brjósti þér?"	"Was no fear in breast yours?"	"Was there no fear in your breast?",
sagði konungur.	said the-king.	said the king.
"Eigi var það",	"None was that".	"That was not so...",
sagði Þorsteinn,	said Thorstein,	said Thorstein,
"því að við hið síðasta ópið skaut mér næsta skelk í bringu".	"then that with the last shriek shot me next-to shivered in chest".	"...because with that last shriek, I nearly shivered in my chest".
Konungur svarar:	The-King answered:	The-king answered:
"Nú skal auka nafn þitt og kalla þig Þorstein skelk héðan af og er hér sverð að eg vil gefa þér að nafnfesti".	"Now shall extra name yours and call you Thorstein shiver from-here of and is here a-sword that i wish to-give to-you as a-nickname".	"Now I shall add an extra name to yours and call you Thorstein Shiver from now on, and here is a sword, that I wish to give you for your nickname".
Þorsteinn þakkaði honum.	Thorstein thanked him.	Thorstein thanked him.
Svo er sagt að Þorsteinn gerðist hirðmaður Ólafs konungs og var með honum síðan og féll á Orminum langa með öðrum köppum konungs.	So was said that Thorstein became court-man Olaf's the-king and was with him since and fell on The-serpent long with other champions the-king's.	And so it was said, that Thorstein became a court man of King Olaf and was with him ever since, until he fell on Olaf's longship 'The Serpent' alongside the king's other champions.

Word List (Old Icelandic to English)

Word List (Old Icelandic to English)

Old Icelandic	English

A, a

að	about, as, at, from, that, then, to
af	from, of, of, out-of
aldrei	never
alla	all, all
allt	all
annað	else
annan	second
annarstaðar	other-places
ansaði	replied
Auðunarsonar	son-of-Audun (name)
augunum	eyes
auka	extra
austur	east

Á, á

á	about, all, from, in, of, on, so, that, the, was, with
áður	before
Ásgeirssonar	son-of-Asgeir (name)

Æ, æ

æðikolls	rage-head
æp	shriek
æpa	shrieking
æpir	cries-out
æpti	shrieked
ætlaði	supposed

B, b

báðum	both
bæ	a-farm
beiddi	needed
beiddist	ask
belgdi	bellowed
best	best
betur	better
bjóst	prepared
blíður	happy
boði	asked
borða	the-table
brá	drew
braut	brought
brennanda	burning
bringu	chest
brjósti	breast
brugðið	custom

D, d

Dólgurinn	the-demon
Drag	drag
draugur	the-demon
draugurinn	the-demon
Drekka	drank
drykkjuborð	drinking-tables
drykkjuborðum	drinking-tables
drýsildjöflanna	petty-devils
duga	be-helped

E, e

eða	but, or
ef	if
eftir	after, following
eg	I, I-am
eigi	no, none, not, not-to
einar	only
einir	alone
einn	a, alone
einrænir	stubborn
Ekki	not
eldinum	the-flames
ella	or-else, otherwise
ellefu	eleven
en	and, but, than, then, when

89

Word List (Old Icelandic to English)

Old Icelandic	English	Old Icelandic	English
engi	no, none	gengur	went
er	as, be, is, it-was, that, was, were, when, which, who, who-was	gerðist	became
		gerir	did
		gólfið	floor, the-floor

F, f

H, h

Old Icelandic	English	Old Icelandic	English
fætur	feet	hafa	had, have
Fáfnisbani	Fafnisbani (name)	hafði	had
fara	go	hann	he, him, it
farið	travelled, went	hans	he, his
fast	fast	Haraldi	Harald (name)
feld	cloak	hátt	high
feldarskautinu	fur-cloak	héðan	from-here
feldinn	cloak	hefir	had, has, has-been
feldinum	cloak	heimilishúss	outhouse, the-outhouse
féll	fell	heitir	named
fer	away	heldur	rather
firn	monstrous	hélt	held
fjandi	a-fiend	helvíti	hell
fjandunum	the-torment	Hér	here
Fjarri	far	herra	lord
fjölmennur	followers	hét	named
flest	most	heyra	be-heard, hear
fór	forwards, went	hið	the
forað	terribly	hilditönn	war-tooth
fram	forwards, from-going, towards	Hinn	he, the
		hirðmaður	court-man
fyrir	before, for	hjá	beside
fyrr	before	hlýða	obey
		hlýddi	obeyed

G, g

		höfði	head
gagn	benefit	höfðuð	had
gamli	old	hófi	measure
ganga	go	hólpinn	to-be-helped
gat	could	höndum	hands
gaul	a-howl	Honum	he, him
gaula	howling	hræ	corpses
gaulað	bellow	hræddist	frightened
gefa	to-give	hræðilega	terribly
gekk	went	hræðslan	afraid
gengið	went	hraustur	brave
gengu	went	hringja	rung
		hús	house

Word List (Old Icelandic to English)

Old Icelandic	English
hvað	how, what
Hvaðan	from-where
hve	how
hver	each, who
Hverja	what
Hverjir	who
Hvers	what
hversu	how-so
hvert	each
Hví	why
hvoftana	cheeks
hvoftunum	cheeks
hvoru	each

I, i

iljarnar	soles-of-the-feet
illa	badly
innstu	the-innermost

Í, í

í	a, about, at, in, of, to
Íslendinga	Icelanders
Íslendingur	the-Icelander
íslenskur	Icelandic

J, j

jafnlítill	as-small
játtaði	agreed
jörðina	the-earth

K, k

kalla	call
kanntu	can-you
kappa	hero
kemur	came
keyra	exceeded
kippir	drew
kirkju	church

Old Icelandic	English
klakklaust	unhurt
klukkan	the-clock
klukkuhljóðið	the-clock-sound
kom	came
komið	come
kominn	come
komst	came
konung	the-king
konungi	the-king
konungs	the-king, the-king's
konungur	the-king
köppum	champions
kvað	asked, be-called, cried-out, said
kveldið	evening, the-evening
kyndarinn	the-kindling
kyndir	kindles

L, l

lá	lay
lagðist	lay
langa	long
lát	let
leið	during, this-way
lengi	long
lengur	long
lét	had
liggur	laid
litið	considered
líttað	a-little

M, m

má	may
maður	a-man, man
mælti	spoke
mátti	may
máttu	might
með	with
megin	may
megum	may
meingerð	offence
meiri	more

Word List (Old Icelandic to English)

Old Icelandic	English
menn	men, the-men
mér	me, to-me
mest	mostly
mesta	most
mig	me
mikið	great, much
mikil	great, much
milli	between
minnsta	quietest
mjög	many, much, very-much
mönnum	men
morgnaði	morning
mundi	would
mundu	will
munduð	would
mundum	would

N, n

Old Icelandic	English
náðir	mercy
nærri	near
næsta	next-to
nafn	name
nafnfesti	a-nickname
nátt	the-night
náttina	night-time, the-night
niður	down
nokkuð	somehow, something
nokkur	some
nokkura	some
nú	now
nýkominn	newly-come

O, o

Old Icelandic	English
ofan	downed
ofn	the-oven
og	and
orða	words
Orminum	the-serpent
oss	to-us

Ó, ó

Old Icelandic	English
ógnarraust	dreadful-voice
Ólafs	Olaf's (name)
Ólafur	Olaf (name)
ómegin	un-mighty
óp	cries-out, shouting
ópi	shrieking
ópið	open, shriek
ósvipt	un-thrown
ótti	fear
óvit	unconscious

Ö, ö

Old Icelandic	English
öðrum	other
ökklaeld	ankle-fire
öskurlega	terribly

P, p

Old Icelandic	English
pína	torment
pínu	torment
písl	torment
píslir	the-torment, torment
púkanum	the-demon
púki	a-demon, demon, the-demon
púkinn	the-demon

R, r

Old Icelandic	English
raknaði	recovered
Reimi	Reim (place)
rekkjufélaga	bed-fellow
rétt	right

S, s

Old Icelandic	English
Sá	so
sæng	the-bed
sængur	bed

Word List (Old Icelandic to English)

Old Icelandic	English
sagði	said
sagðist	said, said
sagður	said
sagt	said
salerni	toilet
saman	together
sat	sat
sátu	sitting
segir	said
segja	say
sem	as, which-is, who
sér	his, saw, them
Sest	sat
setið	sat
setti	put
setu	seat
setur	seats
séuð	seem
síðan	since
síðasta	last
sig	himself
Sigurður	Sigurd (name)
sín	himself
sinn	their
sinnar	his
sitja	sit
sjá	such
sjálfur	himself
skal	shall
skaut	shot
skelk	shiver, shivered
skelmirinn	the-demon
skilja	know
skjótt	quickly
skökuls	shaft
skóm	his-shoes
skyldi	should
slíkum	such
sló	struck
snaraði	snared
sneri	turned
sofa	sleep
sögu	said
spurði	asked
spyrja	ask

Old Icelandic	English
staðnum	the-place
standa	stand
Starkaðar	of-Starkad (name)
Starkaði	Starkad (name)
Starkaður	Starkad (name)
Stendur	stood
steyptist	fell
stóð	stood
stóðu	stood
stórt	a-large
stund	while
sumarið	summer
sundur	down
svaf	slept
svarar	answered
sverð	a-sword
svo	so
sýnir	showed
sýnist	seems

T, t

talað	told
talaði	told
tekur	took
tíðum	often
til	to, to-the
tíma	time
Tók	took

Þ, þ

þá	that, then, there
Það	it, that, to
þaðan	of-there
þakkaði	thanked
þangað	there
þar	that, there
þegi	silent
þegir	silent
þeim	them
þeirra	them
þér	they, to-you, you, yours

Word List (Old Icelandic to English)

Old Icelandic	English	Old Icelandic	English
þess	this	varað	warned
þetta	this	varð	was
þig	you	varðst	were
þitt	yours	varir	aware
þó	then, though	veislu	a-feast
þokað	moved	veislum	feasts
þola	endures	veit	know
þolir	endures	vekja	awake
Þorkell	Thorkel (name)	vel	well
Þorkelsson	son-of-Thorkel (name)	vér	we
Þorstein	Thorstein (name)	vera	be
Þorsteini	Thorstein (name)	verið	been
Þorsteinn	Thorstein (name)	verst	the-worst
þótti	seemed, thought	veturinn	winter
þóttist	thought	við	against, knew, with
þrjár	three	víðara	wider
þú	are-you, you	Víkina	Vik (place)
þunni	thin	vil	will, wish
því	accordingly, as, because, since, then, therefore	vildi	willed
		viltu	will-you
þykir	seems	vissi	knew
þykkvan	thick	víst	certainly
		vita	certainly
		vort	us
		voru	was, were

U, u

um	about, around
undan	further
undrast	wonder
upp	above, up
utan	of

Ú, ú

úr	from, out-of

V, v

vafði	wrapped
vakna	awake
vaknaði	awoke, woke-up
var	aware, then, was, was-with

Y, y

yður	to-you
yðvar	your
yfir	about, over
yminn	the-sound
yrðuð	had-been
ystu	the-outermost

Word List (English to Old Icelandic)

Word List (English to Old Icelandic)

English	*Old Icelandic*
A, a	
a	einn, í
about	á, að, í, um, yfir
above	upp
accordingly	því
a-demon	púki
a-farm	bæ
a-feast	veislu
a-fiend	fjandi
afraid	hræðslan
after	eftir
against	við
agreed	játtaði
a-howl	gaul
a-large	stórt
a-little	líttað
all	á, alla, alla, allt
alone	einir, einn
a-man	maður
and	en, og
a-nickname	nafnfesti
ankle-fire	ökklaeld
answered	svarar
are-you	þú
around	um
as	að, er, sem, því
ask	beiddist, spyrja
asked	boði, kvað, spurði
as-small	jafnlítill
a-sword	sverð
at	að, í
awake	vakna, vekja
aware	var, varir
away	fer
awoke	vaknaði
B, b	
badly	illa
be	er, vera
be-called	kvað
became	gerðist
because	því
bed	sængur
bed-fellow	rekkjufélaga
been	verið
before	áður, fyrir, fyrr
be-heard	heyra
be-helped	duga
bellow	gaulað
bellowed	belgdi
benefit	gagn
beside	hjá
best	best
better	betur
between	milli
both	báðum
brave	hraustur
breast	brjósti
brought	braut
burning	brennanda
but	eða, en
C, c	
call	kalla
came	kemur, kom, komst
can-you	kanntu
certainly	víst, vita
champions	köppum
cheeks	hvoftana, hvoftunum
chest	bringu
church	kirkju
cloak	feld, feldinn, feldinum
come	komið, kominn
considered	litið
corpses	hræ
could	gat
court-man	hirðmaður
cried-out	kvað
cries-out	æpir, óp
custom	brugðið

Word List (English to Old Icelandic)

English	Old Icelandic	English	Old Icelandic
		from-here	héðan
		from-where	Hvaðan
		fur-cloak	feldarskautinu
		further	undan

D, d

English	Old Icelandic
demon	púki
did	gerir
down	niður, sundur
downed	ofan
drag	Drag
drank	Drekka
dreadful-voice	ógnarraust
drew	brá, kippir
drinking-tables	drykkjuborð, drykkjuborðum
during	leið

E, e

English	Old Icelandic
each	hver, hvert, hvoru
east	austur
eleven	ellefu
else	annað
endures	þola, þolir
evening	kveldið
exceeded	keyra
extra	auka
eyes	augunum

F, f

English	Old Icelandic
Fafnisbani (name)	Fáfnisbani
far	Fjarri
fast	fast
fear	ótti
feasts	veislum
feet	fætur
fell	féll, steyptist
floor	gólfið
followers	fjölmennur
following	eftir
for	fyrir
forwards	fór, fram
frightened	hræddist
from	á, að, af, úr
from-going	fram

G, g

English	Old Icelandic
go	fara, ganga
great	mikið, mikil

H, h

English	Old Icelandic
had	hafa, hafði, hefir, höfðuð, lét
had-been	yrðuð
hands	höndum
happy	blíður
Harald (name)	Haraldi
has	hefir
has-been	hefir
have	hafa
he	hann, hans, Hinn, Honum
head	höfði
hear	heyra
held	hélt
hell	helvíti
here	Hér
hero	kappa
high	hátt
him	hann, honum
himself	sig, sín, sjálfur
his	hans, sér, sinnar
his-shoes	skóm
house	hús
how	hvað, hve
howling	gaula
how-so	hversu

I, i

English	Old Icelandic
I	eg
I-am	eg

Word List (English to Old Icelandic)

English	Old Icelandic
Icelanders	Íslendinga
Icelandic	íslenskur
if	ef
in	á, í
is	er
it	hann, Það
it-was	er

K, k

kindles	kyndir
knew	við, vissi
know	skilja, veit

L, l

laid	liggur
last	síðasta
lay	lá, lagðist
let	lát
long	langa, lengi, lengur
lord	herra

M, m

man	maður
many	mjög
may	má, mátti, megin, megum
me	mér, mig
measure	hófi
men	menn, mönnum
mercy	náðir
might	máttu
monstrous	firn
more	meiri
morning	morgnaði
most	flest, mesta
mostly	mest
moved	þokað
much	Mikið, mikil, mjög

English	Old Icelandic

N, n

name	nafn
named	heitir, hét
near	nærri
needed	beiddi
never	aldrei
newly-come	nýkominn
next-to	næsta
night-time	náttina
no	eigi, engi
none	Eigi, Engi
not	eigi, Ekki
not-to	eigi
now	nú

O, o

obey	hlýða
obeyed	hlýddi
of	á, af, af, í, utan
offence	meingerð
of-Starkad (name)	Starkaðar
often	tíðum
of-there	þaðan
Olaf (name)	Ólafur
Olaf's (name)	Ólafs
old	gamli
on	á
only	einar
open	ópið
or	eða
or-else	ella
other	öðrum
other-places	annarstaðar
otherwise	ella
outhouse	heimilishúss
out-of	af, úr
over	yfir

P, p

petty-devils	drýsildjöflanna

Word List (English to Old Icelandic)

English	Old Icelandic
prepared	bjóst
put	setti

Q, q

English	Old Icelandic
quickly	skjótt
quietest	minnsta

R, r

English	Old Icelandic
rage-head	æðikolls
rather	heldur
recovered	raknaði
Reim (place)	Reimi
replied	ansaði
right	rétt
rung	hringja

S, s

English	Old Icelandic
said	kvað, sagði, sagðist, sagðist, sagður, sagt, segir, sögu
sat	sat, Sest, setið
saw	sér
say	segja
seat	setu
seats	setur
second	annan
seem	séuð
seemed	þótti
seems	sýnist, þykir
shaft	skökuls
shall	skal
shiver	skelk
shivered	skelk
shot	skaut
should	skyldi
shouting	óp
showed	sýnir
shriek	æp, ópið
shrieked	æpti
shrieking	æpa, ópi

English	Old Icelandic
Sigurd (name)	Sigurður
silent	þegi, þegir
since	síðan, því
sit	sitja
sitting	sátu
sleep	sofa
slept	svaf
snared	snaraði
so	á, Sá, svo
soles-of-the-feet	iljarnar
some	nokkur, nokkura
somehow	nokkuð
something	nokkuð
son-of-Asgeir (name)	Ásgeirssonar
son-of-Audun (name)	Auðunarsonar
son-of-Thorkel (name)	Þorkelsson
spoke	mælti
stand	standa
Starkad (name)	Starkaði, Starkaður
stood	Stendur, stóð, stóðu
struck	sló
stubborn	einrænir
such	sjá, slíkum
summer	sumarið
supposed	ætlaði

T, t

English	Old Icelandic
terribly	forað, hræðilega, öskurlega
than	en
thanked	þakkaði
that	á, að, er, þá, það, þar
the	á, hið, hinn
the-bed	sæng
the-clock	klukkan
the-clock-sound	klukkuhljóðið
the-demon	Dólgurinn, draugur, draugurinn, púkanum, púki, púkinn, skelmirinn
the-earth	jörðina
the-evening	kveldið
the-flames	eldinum

Word List (English to Old Icelandic)

English	Old Icelandic
the-floor	gólfið
the-Icelander	Íslendingur
the-innermost	innstu
their	sinn
the-kindling	kyndarinn
the-king	konung, konungi, konungs, konungur
the-king's	konungs
them	sér, þeim, þeirra
the-men	menn
then	að, en, þá, þó, því, var
the-night	nátt, náttina
the-outermost	ystu
the-outhouse	heimilishúss
the-oven	ofn
the-place	staðnum
there	þá, þangað, þar
therefore	því
the-serpent	Orminum
the-sound	yminn
the-table	borða
the-torment	fjandunum, píslir
the-worst	verst
they	þér
thick	þykkvan
thin	þunni
this	þess, þetta
this-way	leið
Thorkel (name)	Þorkell
Thorstein (name)	Þorstein, Þorsteini, Þorsteinn
though	þó
thought	þótti, þóttist
three	þrjár
time	tíma
to	að, í, það, til
to-be-helped	hólpinn
together	saman
to-give	gefa
toilet	salerni
told	talað, talaði
to-me	mér
took	tekur, Tók
torment	pína, pínu, písl, píslir
to-the	til
to-us	oss
towards	fram
to-you	þér, yður
travelled	farið
turned	sneri

U, u

English	Old Icelandic
unconscious	óvit
unhurt	klakklaust
un-mighty	ómegin
un-thrown	ósvipt
up	upp
us	vort

V, v

English	Old Icelandic
very-much	mjög
Vik (place)	Víkina

W, w

English	Old Icelandic
warned	varað
war-tooth	hilditönn
was	á, er, var, varð, voru
was-with	var
we	vér
well	vel
went	farið, fór, gekk, gengið, gengu, gengur
were	er, varðst, voru
what	Hvað, Hverja, Hvers
when	En, er
which	er
which-is	sem
while	stund
who	er, Hver, Hverjir, sem
who-was	er
why	Hví
wider	víðara
will	mundu, vil
willed	vildi

Word List (English to Old Icelandic)

English   *Old Icelandic*

will-you   viltu
winter   veturinn
wish   vil
with   á, með, við
woke-up   vaknaði
wonder   undrast
words   orða
would   mundi, munduð, mundum
wrapped   vafði

Y, y

you   þér, þig, þú
your   yðvar
yours   þér, þitt

A Word Comparison of Old Norse and Old Icelandic Words

A Word Comparison of Old Norse and Old Icelandic Words

Old Norse	Old Icelandic	English	Old Norse	Old Icelandic	English
áðr	áður	before	hraustr	hraustur	brave
æpði	æpti	shrieked	hváftana	hvoftana	cheeks
ætlaða	ætlaði	supposed	hváftunum	hvoftunum	cheeks
aldri	aldrei	never	hvárum	hvoru	each
annat	annað	else	hvat	hvað	how
anzaði	ansaði	replied	hvat	hvað	what
at	að	about	hvé	hve	how
at	að	as	hverir	hverjir	who
at	að	at	hverr	hver	each
at	að	from	hverr	hver	who
at	að	that	inn	hinn	the
at	að	then	íslendingr	íslendingur	the-Icelander
at	að	to	íslenzkr	íslenskur	Icelandic
austr	austur	east	it	hið	the
belgði	belgdi	bellowed	játaði	játtaði	agreed
betr	betur	better	kemr	kemur	came
bezt	best	best	klaklaust	klakklaust	unhurt
blíðr	blíður	happy	klukkuhljóðit	klukkuhljóðið	the-clock-sound
brugðit	brugðið	custom	kom	komst	came
dólgrinn	dólgurinn	the-demon	komit	komið	come
draugr	draugur	the-demon	konungr	konungur	the-king
draugrinn	draugurinn	the-demon	kveldit	kveldið	evening
ek	eg	I	kveldit	kveldið	the-evening
ek	eg	I-am	lengr	lengur	long
ellifu	ellefu	eleven	liggr	liggur	laid
fætr	fætur	feet	litit	litið	considered
farit	farið	travelled	lítt	líttað	a-little
farit	farið	went	maðr	maður	a-man
fell	féll	fell	maðr	maður	man
ferr	fer	away	mik	mig	me
fjölmennr	fjölmennur	followers	mikit	mikið	great
fjöndunum	fjandunum	the-torment	mikit	mikið	much
foraðs	forað	terribly	mjök	mjög	many
gaulat	gaulað	bellow	mjök	mjög	much
gengit	gengið	went	mjök	mjög	very-much
gengr	gengur	went	mundið	munduð	would
gólfit	gólfið	floor	mundim	mundum	would
gólfit	gólfið	the-floor	niðr	niður	down
héðan	héðan	from-here	nökkura	nokkura	some
heldr	heldur	rather	nökkurr	nokkur	some
helt	hélt	held	nökkut	nokkuð	somehow
hirðmaðr	hirðmaður	court-man	nökkut	nokkuð	something
hræðiliga	hræðilega	terribly	ok	og	and

A Word Comparison of Old Norse and Old Icelandic Words

Old Norse	Old Icelandic	English
öklaeld	ökklaeld	ankle-fire
Óláfr	Ólafur	Olaf (name)
Óláfs	Ólafs	Olaf's (name)
ópit	ópið	open
ópit	ópið	shriek
ór	úr	from
ór	úr	out-of
öskurliga	öskurlega	terribly
Reinu	Reimi	Reim (place)
sængr	sængur	bed
sagðr	sagður	said
séð	séuð	seem
setit	setið	sat
sezt	sest	sat
Sigurðr	Sigurður	Sigurd (name)
sik	sig	himself
sjálfr	sjálfur	himself
Starkaðr	Starkaður	Starkad (name)
stendr	stendur	stood
steypðist	steyptist	fell
sumarit	sumarið	summer
sundr	sundur	down
svá	svo	so
talat	talað	told
tekr	tekur	took
þangat	þangað	there
þat	það	it
þat	það	that
þat	það	to
þeira	þeirra	them
þik	þig	you
þokat	þokað	moved
Þorsteirm	Þorsteinn	Thorstein (name)
þóttumst	þóttist	thought
þykkir	þykir	seems
undrumst	undrast	wonder
útan	utan	of
vaknaða	vaknaði	woke-up
varat	varað	warned
varð	varðst	were
varr	var	aware
várt	vort	us
váru	voru	was
váru	voru	were

Old Norse	Old Icelandic	English
veizlu	veislu	a-feast
veizlum	veislum	feasts
verit	verið	been
vetrinn	veturinn	winter
villtu	viltu	will-you
vissa	vissi	knew
vit	við	knew
yðr	yður	to-you
yrðið	yrðuð	had-been
yztu	ystu	the-outermost

The Tale of Thiðrandi and Thórhall (*Old Norse*)

Old Norse	Literal	English
1	**1**	**1**
Þórhallr hét maðr norrœnn;	Thorhall was-named a-man northern;	There was a nordic man named Thorhall.
hann kom út til Íslands á dögum Hákonar jarls Sigurðarsonar.	he came out to Iceland in the-days-of Hakon the-earl Sigurdson.	He came out to Iceland in the days of earl Hakon Sigurdson.
Hann tók land í Sýrlœkjarósi, ok bjó á Hörgslandi.	He took land in Syrlaekjaros, and settled at Horgsland.	He took land in Syrlaekjaros and settled at Horgsland.
Þórhallr var fróðr maðr ok mjök framsýnn, ok var kallaðr Þórhallr spámaðr.	Thorhall was a-wise man and much far-sighted, and was called Thorhall the-Seer.	Thorhall was a wise man and very far-sighted, and he was called Thorhall the Seer
Þórhallr spámaðr bjó þá á Hörgslandi, er Síðu-Hallr bjó at Hofi í Álftafirði, ok var með þeim hin mesta vinátta.	Thorhall the-Seer settled then at Horgsland, when Sidu-Hall settled at Hof in Alftafjord, and was with them the most friendship.	Thorhall the Seer then settled at Horgsland when Sidu-Hall settled at Hof in Alftafjord and between them was the best friendship.
Gisti Hallr á Hörgslandi hvert sumar, er hann reið til þings.	Guested Hall at Horgsland each summer, as he rode to the-assembly.	Hall was a guest at Horgsland each summer as he ridden to the assembly.
Þórhallr fór ok oft til heimboða austr þangat, ok var þar löngum.	Thorhall travelled also often to home-invitation east from-there, and was there long.	Thorhall also travelled by invitation to the east and spent a long time there.
Sonr Halls hinn elzti hét Þiðrandi;	Son Hall's the eldest was-named Thidrandi;	Hall's eldest son was named Thidrand.
hann var manna vænstr ok efniligastr;	he was a-man handsome and promising;	He was a handsom and promising man.
unni Hallr honum mest allra sona sinna.	loved Hall him the-most of-all sons his.	Hall loved him the most of all his sons.
Þiðrandi fór landa í milli, þegar hann hafði aldr til.	Thidrandi travelled the-lands in between, once he had age to.	Thidrand travelled between lands as soon as he was old enough.

The Tale of Thiðrandi and Thórhall (Old Norse)

Old Norse	Literal	English
Hann var hinn vinsælasti, hvar sem hann kom, því at hann var hinn mesti atgervismaðr, lítillátr ok blíðr við hvert barn.	He was most endearing, where that he came, for that he was the most accomplished, modest and gentle with every child.	He was most endearing wherever he came, for he was the most accomplished but modest, and gentle with every man and child.
Þat var eitt sumar, at Hallr bauð Þórhalli vin sínum austr þangat, þá er hann reið af þingi.	It was one summer, that Hall invited Thorhall friend his east from-there, then when he was-riding from the-assembly.	It happened one summer that Hall invited Thorhall his friend to the east when he was riding home from the assembly.
Þórhallr fór austr nökkuru síðar enn Hallr, ok tók Hallr við honum sem jafnan með hin mesta blíðskap.	Thorhall travelled east sometime later than Hall, and took Hall with him as usual with the greatest kindness.	Thorhall travelled east sometime later than Hall, and Hall received him with with the greatest kindness as usual.
Dvaldist Þórhallr þar um sumarit, ok sagði Hallr, at hann skyldi eigi fyrri fara heim enn lokit væri haustboði.	Dwelled Thorhall there about summer, and said Hall, that he should not before travel home than ended the-home autumn-feast.	Thorhall dwelled there over the summer and Hall said that he should not travel home before the autumn feast had ended.

2

Þat sumar kom Þiðrandi út í Berufirði.	That summer came Thidrandi out to Berufjord.	That summer Thidrand came out to Berufjord.
Þá var hann átján vetra.	Then was he eighteen winters.	Then he was 18 winters old.
Fór hann heim til föður síns.	Travelled he home to father his.	He travelled home to his father.
Dáðust menn þá enn mjök at honum sem oft áðr, ok lofuðu atgervi hans; enn Þórhallr spámaðr þagði jafnan, þá er menn lofuðu hann mest.	Admired people then as much of him as often before, and praised deeds his; but Thorhall the-Seer silent always, then when people praised him the-most.	People admired him as much as before and praised his deeds, but Thorhall the Seer was always silent when people praised him the most.
Þá spurði Hallr, hví þat sætti,	Then asked Hall, what the reason,	Then Hall asked what the reason was for this:
"er þú leggr svá fátt til um hagi sonar míns Þiðranda? því at mér þykkir þat merkilegt, er þú mælir, Þórhallr", segir hann.	"are you suggesting so little to about health son mine Thidrandi? because that I think it remarkable, that-which you say, Thorhall", said he.	"because I think that whatever you say Thorhall is always remarkable to me", he said.
Þórhallr svaraði:	Thorhall answered:	Thorhall answered:

The Tale of Thiðrandi and Thórhall (Old Norse)

Old Norse	Literal	English
"Eigi gengr mér þat til þess, at mér mislíki nökkurr hlutr við hann eðr þik, eðr ek sjái síðr enn aðrir menn, at hann er hinn merkilegasti maðr, heldr berr hitt til, at margir verða til at lofa hann, ok hefir hann marga hluti til þess, þó at hann virði sik lítils sjálfr.	"Not goes to-me that to this, that I mislike some part with him or you, or-that I see less than other people, that he is the-most remarkable man, but bears others to, that many become until to praise him, and has he many things to this, although that he values himself little of-himself.	"It does not occur to me that I dislike anything about him or you, or that I see less than other men that he is the most remarkable man, but rather that many will praise him and he has many things to do with it, although he values himself little.
Kann þat vera, at hans njóti eigi lengi, ok mun þér þá œrin eftirsjá at um son þinn svá vel mannaðan, þó at eigi lofi allir menn fyrir þér hans atgervi".	Can it be, that he enjoys not for-long, and should you then mad look-back that about son yours so well manned, though that not praise all people for to-you his deeds".	It may be that he will not enjoy it for long, and then you will regret that your son is so well mannered, even though not all people praise you for his deeds".
Enn er á leið sumarit tók Þórhallr mjök at ógleðjast.	When was that passed summer took Thorhall much to ungladness.	When that summer was passed, Thorhall took much sadness.
Hallr spurði, hví þat sætti.	Hall asked, what the reason.	Hall asked what the reason was.
Þórhallr svarar:	Thorhall answered:	Thorhall answered:
"Illt hygg ek til haustboðs þessa, er hér skal vera, því at mér býðr þat fyrir, at spámaðr mun vera drepinn at þessi veizlu".	"Ill think I to autumn-harvest this, that here shall be, for to me invited it for, that a-seer shall be killed at this feast".	"I think evil of this autumn invitation which is to be here, for it offers me that a prophet will be killed at this feast".
"Þar kann ek at gera grein á", segir bóndi;	"Here can I that make explanation of", said the-farmer;	"I can explain that," said the farmer.
"ek á uxa einn, tíu vetra gamlan, þann er ek kalla spámann, því at hann er spakari enn flest naut önnur.	"I have ox one, ten winters old, that which I call the-Seer, because that he is wiser than most bulls others.	"I have a ten-year-old ox, whom I call the Prophet, for he is wiser than most other bulls.

The Tale of Thiðrandi and Thórhall (Old Norse)

Old Norse	Literal	English
Enn hann gkal drepa at haustboðinu, ok þarf þik þetta eigi at ógleðja, því at ek ætla, at þessi mín veizla sem aðrar skuli þér ok öðrum vinum mínum verða til sœmdar".	But he shall be-killed at autumn-feast, and need you this not be saddened, because that I suppose, that this my feast as others shall you and other friends mine be to honour".	But he will be killed at the autumn feast, and you need not be saddened because of this, for I think that this feast of mine, as well as others, will be an honour to you and to my other friends".
Þórhallr svarar:	Thorhall answered:	Thorhall answered:
"Ek fann þetta ok eigi af því til, at ek væra hræddr um mitt líf, ok boðar mér fyrir meiri tíðindi ok undarligri, þau er ek mun at sinni eigi upp kveða".	"I found this and not of because to, that I was scared about my life, and proclaims to-me for greater tidings and stranger, than is I may to mind not up speak".	"I found this not because I was afraid of my life, but because it proclaims to me more tidings and stranger ones that I have a mind not to speak up about".
Hallr mælti:	Hall said:	Hallur said:
"Þá er ok ekki fyrir at bregða boði því".	"Then is and not for that break to-break therefore".	"Then there is no way to break the offer".
Þórhallr svarar:	Thorhall answered:	Þórhallur answered:
"Ekki mun tjóa at gera þat, því at þat mun fram ganga sem ætlat er".	"Not would that be that the-matter, therefore that it should from going as intended be".	"It will not do in this matter because it will go as intended".

3

Veizlan var nú búin at vetrnóttum.	The-feast was prepared that winter-night.	The feast was prepared for the winter nights.
Kom þar fátt boðsmanna, því at veðr var hvasst ok viðgerðar-mikit.	Came there few invited-men, because the weather was stormy and widely-made-much.	Few of the invited people came because the weather was stormy and difficult to travel in.
Enn er menn settust tilborðs um kveldit, þá mælti Þórhallr:	When were the-people sat to-the-tables about evening, then spoke Thorhall:	When the people sat at the tables in the evening then Thorhall spoke:

The Tale of Thiðrandi and Thórhall (Old Norse)

Old Norse	Literal	English
"Biðja vilda ek, at menn hefði ráð mín um þat, at engi maðr komi hér út á þessi nótt, því at mikil mein munu hér á liggja, ef af þessu er brugðit, og hverigir hlutir, sem verða í bendingum, gefi menn eigi gaum at, því at illu mun furða, ef nökkurr anzar til".	"Ask will I, that people have advice mine about it, that no man comes here outside on this night, for that much harm shall here to lay, if of this is broken, and whatever things, which happen as signs, give people not heed to, for that evil shall follow, if anyone responds to".	"I wish to ask that people hear my advice that no man goes outside on this night, for there shall be much harm if this is broken and whatever things people might see as signs are to be given no heed to, for evil shall follow if anyone answers".
Hallr bað menn halda orð Þórhalls;	Hall asked people hold words Thorhall's;	Hall asked people to hold to Thorhall's words:
"því at þau rjúfast ekki", segir hann,	"because that they break not", said he,	"because they will not break", he said,
"ok er um heilt bezt at búa".	"and is about wholly best to prepare".	"and it will be best to be wholly prepared".
Þiðrandi gekk um beina;	Thidrandi went about assisting;	Thidrand went about assisting.
var hann í því sem öðru mjúkr ok lítillátr.	was he as then as-in other-things humble and modest.	He was as in other things humble and modest.
Enn er menn gengu at sofa, þá skipaði Þiðrandi gestum í sæng sína; enn hann sló sér niðr í sæti yztr við þili.	But when people went to sleep, then directed Thidrandi guests to bed his; but he laid-out himself down on a-bench outer with wall.	But when people went to sleep Thidrand directed guests to his bed and he laid himself down on a bench at the outermost wall.
Enn er flestir menn váru sofnaðir, þá var kvatt dyra, ok lét engi maðr sem vissi.	When that most people were sleeping, then was summons at-the-door, and had no man as-if knew.	When most people were asleep there was a summons at the door, but no man acted as if they knew of it.
Fór svá þrisvar.	Came so three-times.	It came three times.
Þá spratt Þiðrandi upp, ok mælti:	Then sprang Thidrandi up, and spoke:	Then Thidrand sprang up and spoke:
"Þetta er skömm mikil, er menn láta hér allir sem sofi, ok munu boðsmenn komnir".	"This is a-shame great, that people let here all who sleep, and shall-be invited-men coming".	"This is a great shame that the people here are asleep and these must be guests coming".
Hann tók sverð í hönd sér, ok gekk út;	He took sword in hand his, and went out;	He took his sword in his hand and went out.
hann sá engan mann.	he saw no person.	He saw no person.

The Tale of Thiðrandi and Thórhall (Old Norse)

Old Norse	Literal	English
Honum kom þá þat í hug, at nökkurir boðsmenn myndi hafa riðit fyrr heim til bœjar, ok riðit síðan aftr í móti þeim, er seinna riðu,	To-him came then that a thought, that some invited-men would have rode for the-house to the-town, and rode afterwards back to meet them, that later rode,	A thought came to him that some guests would have ridden to the house and then back to the town to meet those who had ridden behind them arriving later.
Hann gekk þá undir viðköstinn, ok heyrði, at riðit var norðan á völlinn.	He went then under the-wood-pile, and heard, that riding was north into the-field.	He walked under the wood pile and heard the sound of riding coming from the north into the field.
Hann sá, at þat varu konur níu, ok allar í svörtum klæðum, ok höfðu brugðin sverð í höndum.	He saw, that it was women nine, and all in black clothes, and had drawn-out swords in hand.	He saw that there were nine women and they were all in black clothes and had drawn swords in their hands.
Hann heyrði ok at riðit var sunnan á völlinn,	He heard also that riding was from-the-south into the-field,	He also heard the sound of riding coming from the south into the field.
þar váru ok níu konur, allar í ljósum klæðum ok á hvítum hestum.	there were also nine women, all in bright clothes and on white horses.	There were also nine women, all in bright clothes and on white horses.
Þá vildi Þiðrandi snúa inn, ok segja mönnum sýnina; enn þá bar at konurnar fyrr, hinar svartklæddu, ok sóttu at honum; enn hann varðist drengiliga.	Then willed Thidrandi to-return inside, and say-to the-men this-sight; but then bore to the-women before, the black-clothes, and set-about to him; and he defended bravely.	Then Thidrand wished to return inside and tell the men of what he had seen, but then the women in the black clothes came upon him first and set about him, and he defended himself bravely.
Enn langri stundu síðar vaknaði Þórhallr, ok spurði, hvárt Þiðrandi vekti, ok var honum eigi svarat.	Then a-long while later woke Thorhall, and asked, whether Thidrandi awoke, and was he not answered.	A long while later Thorhall woke and asked whether Thidrand was awake but he was not answered.
Þórhallr kvað þá mundu of seinat.	Thorhall cried then would-be too-late.	Thorhall cried out that it would be too late.

4

Var þá út gengit;	Were they out going;	They went outside.

The Tale of Thiðrandi and Thórhall (Old Norse)

Old Norse	Literal	English
var á tunglskin ok frostviðri.	was it moonlight and frosty.	It was moonlight and frosty.
Þeir fundu Þiðranda liggja særðan, ok var hann borinn inn.	They found Thidrandi lying wounded, and was he carried inside.	They found Thidrand lying wounded and was he carried inside.
Ok er menn höfðu orð við hann, sagði hann þetta allt, sem fyrir hann hafði borit.	And when people had words with him, told he this all, that before he had bore.	And when the people had gotten word from him, he told them all that had happened before.
Hann andaðist þann sama morgun í lýsing, ok var lagðr í haug at heiðnum sið.	He died that same morning at daybreak, and was laid in a-mound as heathen tradition.	He died that same morning at daybreak and was laid in a mound as in the heathen tradition.
Síðan var haldit fréttum um mannaferðir, ok vissu menn ekki vánir óvina Þiðranda,	Later was held news about people's-travels, and knew people not the-hopes enemies-of Thidrandi,	Later there was news of peoples' travels and people did not know the hopes of Thidrand's enemies.
Hallr spurði Þórhall, hverju gegna myndi um þenna undarliga atburð.	Hall asked Thorhall, how going would about these strange events.	Hall asked Thorhall how these strange events would turn out.
Þórhallr svarar:	Thorhall answered:	Thorhall answered:
"Þat veit ek eigi; enn geta má ek til, at þetta hafi engar konur verit aðrar enn fylgjur yðrar frænda.	"That know I not; but guess may I to, that this have no women been other than followers your kinsmen.	"That I do not know, but I guess that these women can only have been followers of your kinsmen.
Get ek, at hér eftir komi siðaskifti, ok mun því næst koma siðr betri hingat til lands.	Guess I, that here after comes conversion, and should therefore next come a-custom better here to the-land.	I guess that there shall come a conversion, and there will be a better custom here to the land.
Ætla ek þær dísir yðrar, er fylgt hafa þessum átrúnaði, munu hafa vitat fyrir siðaskifti, ok þat, at þér munit verða þeim afhendir frændr.	Suppose I there spirits yours, were followers having this religion, would have known beforehand the-conversion, and it, that you shall come-to them rejected kinsmen.	I suppose that these spirits of you who have followed the old faith would have known beforehand about this conversion, and that they would be rejected by your kinsmen.
Nú munu þær eigi hafa því unat, at hafa engan skatt af yðr áðr, ok munu þær því hann haft hafa í sinn hlut;	Now shall they not have therefore liked, to have no tribute from you before, and would there that have in their lot;	Now they will not have liked to have had no tribute from you before and they would therefore have their lot.

The Tale of Thiðrandi and Thórhall (Old Norse)

Old Norse	Literal	English
enn hinar betri dísir mundri hafa viljat hjálpa honum, ok komust eigi við at svá búnu.	but the better spirits would will to-help him, and they-came not with to so good.	But the better spirits would have wished to help him, but they did not arrive in time.
Nú munut þér frændr þeira njóta, er þann hinn ókunna sið munut hafa, er þær boða fyrir ok fylgja".	Now shall you kinsmen of-them enjoy, which then shall have, what they preach for and follow".	Now your kinsmen shall enjoy the help of them by following what they preach for".

5

Old Norse	Literal	English
Nú boðaði þessi atburðr fyrir, sem Þórhallr sagði, ok margir hlutir þvílíkir, þann fagnaðartíma, sem eftir kom, at allsvaldandi Guði virðist at líta miskunnaraugum á þann lýð, er Ísland byggði, ok leysa þar fólk fyrir sína erindreka af löngum fjandans þrældómi, ok leiða síðan til samlags eilífrar erfðar sinna œskilegra sona, sem hann hefir fyrir heitit, alla þá, er honum vilja trúlega þjóna með staðfesti góðra verka;	Now foretold this event for, which Thorhall said, and many things like, that celebrated-time, which afterwards came, to omnipotent God seeming to look mercifully to that people, of Iceland settled, and redeemed that folk for their ambassadors of long damned slavery, and lead afterwards to union eternal inherited his desirable sons, whom he has before promised, all those, who him will truely serve with steadfast good works;	Now this event was foretold which Thorhall had said many things about, the celebrated time which came afterwards, an omnipotent god seeing and looking mercifully to the people that settled Iceland, redeeming the people from their ambassadors of long and damned slavery, leading afterwards to an eternal union, inherited by his desirable sons, that he has promised to all those who will truly serve him with steadfast good works.
svá ok eigi síðr sýndi óvinr alls mannkyns opinberliga í slíkum hlutum ok mörgum öðrum, þeim er í frásagnir eru fœrðir, hversu nauðigr hann lét laust sitt ránfengi ok þann lýð, er hann hafði áðr allan tíma haldit hertekinn í villuböndum sinna bölvuðu skurðgoða, þá er hann hvessti með slíkum áhlaupum sína grimdarfulla reiði á þeim, sem hann hafði vald yfir, sem hann vissi nálgast sína skömm ok makligan skaða síns herfangs.	so and no less it-seemed enemies all mankind publicly in such things and many others, they are of stories are told, how compelled he to-have without this robbery and that people, that he had before all time stayed captive of sins theirs cursed idols, then when he hissed with such raids his cruelty-full anger at them, which he had power over, which he knew approached their shame and make-like damage his war-takings.	So and it seemed no less that the enemies of all mankind publicly and in such things and many others, of which there are stories told of how they were compelled to abandon robbery, and the people that had before remained captive of the sins of their cursed idols when they hissed with such brutality and cruelty-full anger at those which they had power over, of which they knew they approached their shame, and the damage of their war-takings.

The Tale of Thiðrandi and Thórhall (Old Norse)

Old Norse	Literal	English
6	**6**	**6**
Enn Halli þótti svá mikit lát Þiðranda sonar síns, at hann undi eigi lengr at búa at Hofi;	But Hall thought so much had Thidrandi son his, that he on not longer to live at Hof;	But Halli thought so much of his son Thidrand's death that he could no longer live at Hof.
færði hann þá byggð sína til Þváttár.	brought he then settlement his to Thvatta.	He then moved his settlement to Thvatta.
Þat var einn tíma at Þváttá, þá er Þórhallr spámaðr var þar at heimboði með Halli, (at)	It was one time at Thvatta, then that Thorhall the-Seer was there at home-invitation with Hall, ()	There was a time at Thvatta when Thorhall the Seer was invited to stay with Hall.
Hallr lá í hvílugólfi ok Þórhallr í annarri rekkju; enn gluggr var á hvílugólfinu.	Hall lay in bed-closet and Thorhall in another bed; which window was on a-bed-closet.	Hall lay in a bed-closet and Thorhall in another bed-closet which had a window.
Ok einn morgin, er þeir vöktu báðir, þá brosti Þórhallr.	And one morning, when they woke both, then burst-out-laughing Thorhall.	And one morning they both woke and then Thorhall burst out laughing.
Hallr mælti:	Hall spoke:	Hall spoke:
"Hví brosir þú nú?"	"Why laughing are-you now?"	"Why are you laughing now?"
Þórhallr svarar:	Thorhall answered:	Thorhall answered:
"At því brosi ek, at margr hóll opnast, ok hvert kvikindi býr sinn bagga, bæði smá ok stór, ok gera fardaga".	"That because-of laughing am-I, that many hills they-open, and every creature prepares their bags, both small and great, and making moving-day".	"I am laughing because many hills are opening, and every creature prepares their bags, both small and great, and does their moving-day".
Ok litlu síðar urðu þau tíðindi, sem nú skal frá segja:	And little later came there the-news, that now shall from be-said:	And a little while later there came the news that shall now be said from.
(þ.e. kristniboð Þangbrands prests á Íslandi).	(i.e. christian-message Thangbrand priest in Iceland).	(i.e. The Christian message of Thangbrand the priest in Iceland).

Word List (Old Norse to English)

Old Norse	English
A, a	
aðrar	other, others
aðrir	other
af	from, from, of, of
afhendir	rejected
aftr	back
aldr	age
alla	all
allan	all
allar	all
allir	all, all
allra	of-all
alls	all
allsvaldandi	omnipotent
allt	all
andaðist	died
annarri	another
anzar	responds
at	as, at, at, be, be, of, that, that, the, to, to, 0
atburð	events
atburðr	event
atgervi	deeds
atgervismaðr	accomplished
austr	east, east
Á, á	
á	at, have, in, into, it, of, on, that, to
áðr	before
áhlaupum	raids
álftafirði	Alftafjord (place)
átján	eighteen
átrúnaði	religion
Æ, æ	
ætla	suppose
ætlat	intended

Old Norse	English
B, b	
bað	asked
báðir	both
bæði	both
bagga	bags
bar	bore
barn	child
bauð	invited
beina	assisting
bendingum	signs
berr	bears
berufirði	Berufjord (place)
betri	better
bezt	best
biðja	ask
bjó	settled
blíðr	gentle
blíðskap	kindness
boða	preach
boðaði	foretold
boðar	proclaims
boði	to-break
boðsmanna	invited-men
boðsmenn	invited-men
bœjar	the-town
bölvuðu	cursed
bóndi	the-farmer
borinn	carried
borit	bore
bregða	break
brosi	laughing
brosir	laughing
brosti	burst-out-laughing
brugðin	drawn-out
brugðit	broken
búa	live, prepare
búin	prepared
búnu	good
býðr	invited
byggð	settlement
byggði	settled
býr	prepares

112

Word List (Old Norse to English)

Old Norse	English

D, d

Old Norse	English
dáðust	admired
dísir	spirits
dögum	the-days-of
drengiliga	bravely
drepa	be-killed
drepinn	killed
dvaldist	dwelled
dyra	at-the-door

E, e

Old Norse	English
eðr	or, or-that
ef	if
efniligastr	promising
eftir	after, afterwards
eftirsjá	look-back
eigi	no, not
eilífrar	eternal
einn	one
eitt	one
ek	am-I, I
ekki	not
elzti	eldest
engan	no
engar	no
engi	no
enn	and, as, but, than, then, when, which
er	are, as, be, is, of, that, that-which, was, were, what, when, which, who
erfðar	inherited
erindreka	ambassadors
eru	are

F, f

Old Norse	English
fagnaðartíma	celebrated-time
fann	found
fara	travel
fardaga	moving-day
fátt	few, little
fjandans	damned
flest	most
flestir	most
föður	father
fœrði	brought
fœrðir	told
fólk	folk
fór	came, travelled
frá	from
frænda	kinsmen
frændr	kinsmen
fram	from
framsýnn	far-sighted
frásagnir	stories
fréttum	news
fróðr	a-wise
frostviðri	frosty
fundu	found
furða	follow
fylgja	follow
fylgjur	followers
fylgt	followers
fyrir	before, beforehand, for
fyrr	before, for
fyrri	before

G, g

Old Norse	English
gamlan	old
ganga	going
gaum	heed
gefi	give
gegna	going
gekk	went
gengit	going
gengr	goes
gengu	went
gera	make, making, that
gestum	guests
get	guess
geta	guess
gisti	guested

Word List (Old Norse to English)

Old Norse	English
gkal	shall
gluggr	window
góðra	good
grein	explanation
grimdarfulla	cruelty-full
guði	god

H, h

Old Norse	English
hafa	have, having, will
hafði	had
hafi	have
haft	that
hagi	health
hákonar	Hakon (name)
halda	hold
haldit	held, stayed
halli	Hall (name)
hallr	Hall (name)
halls	Hall's (name)
hann	he, him, 0
hans	he, his
haug	a-mound
haustboði	autumn-feast
haustboðinu	autumn-feast
haustboðs	autumn-harvest
hefði	have
hefir	has
heiðnum	heathen
heilt	wholly
heim	home, the-house
heimboða	home-invitation
heimboði	home-invitation
heitit	promised
heldr	but
hér	here
herfangs	war-takings
hertekinn	captive
hestum	horses
hét	was-named
heyrði	heard
hin	the
hinar	the
hingat	here
hinn	most, the, the-most, 0

Old Norse	English
hitt	others
hjálpa	to-help
hlut	lot
hluti	things
hlutir	things
hlutr	part
hlutum	things
höfðu	had
hofi	Hof (place)
hóll	hills
hönd	hand
höndum	hand
honum	he, him, to-him
hörgslandi	Horgsland (place)
hræddr	scared
hug	thought
hvar	where
hvárt	whether
hvasst	stormy
hverigir	whatever
hverju	how
hversu	how
hvert	each, every
hvessti	hissed
hví	what, why
hvílugólfi	bed-closet
hvílugólfinu	a-bed-closet
hvítum	white
hygg	think

I, i

Old Norse	English
illt	ill
illu	evil
inn	inside

Í, í

Old Norse	English
í	a, as, at, in, of, on, to
ísland	Iceland (place)
íslandi	Iceland (place)
íslands	Iceland (place)

Word List (Old Norse to English)

Old Norse	English

J, j

jafnan	always, usual
jarls	the-earl

K, k

kalla	call
kallaðr	called
kann	can
klæðum	clothes
kom	came
koma	come
komi	comes
komnir	coming
komust	they-came
konur	women
konurnar	the-women
kristniboð	christian-message
kvað	cried
kvatt	summons
kveða	speak
kveldit	evening
kvikindi	creature

L, l

lá	lay
lagðr	laid
land	land
landa	the-lands
lands	the-land
langri	a-long
lát	had
láta	let
laust	without
leggr	suggesting
leið	passed
leiða	lead
lengi	for-long
lengr	longer
lét	had, to-have
leysa	redeemed
líf	life
liggja	lay, lying
líta	look
lítillátr	modest
lítils	little
litlu	little
ljósum	bright
lofa	praise
lofi	praise
lofuðu	praised
lokit	ended
löngum	long
lýð	people
lýsing	daybreak

M, m

má	may
maðr	a-man, man
mælir	say
mælti	said, spoke
makligan	make-like
mann	person
manna	a-man
mannaðan	manned
mannaferðir	people's-travels
mannkyns	mankind
marga	many
margir	many
margr	many
með	with
mein	harm
meiri	greater
menn	people, the-people
mér	I, me, to-me
merkilegasti	remarkable
merkilegt	remarkable
mest	the-most
mesta	greatest, most
mesti	most
mikil	great, much
mikit	much
milli	between
mín	mine, my
míns	mine

Word List (Old Norse to English)

Old Norse	English
mínum	mine
miskunnaraugum	mercifully
mislíki	mislike
mitt	my
mjök	much
mjúkr	humble
mönnum	the-men
morgin	morning
mörgum	many
morgun	morning
móti	meet
mun	may, shall, should, would
mundri	would
mundu	would-be
munit	shall
munu	shall, shall-be, would
munut	shall
myndi	would

N, n

Old Norse	English
næst	next
nálgast	approached
nauðigr	compelled
naut	bulls
niðr	down
níu	nine
njóta	enjoy
njóti	enjoys
nökkurir	some
nökkurr	anyone, some
nökkuru	sometime
norðan	north
norrœnn	northern
nótt	night
nú	now, 0

O, o

Old Norse	English
of	too-late
oft	often
og	and
ok	also, and
opinberliga	publicly
opnast	they-open
orð	words

Ó, ó

Old Norse	English
ógleðja	saddened
ógleðjast	ungladness
ókunna	0
óvina	enemies-of
óvinr	enemies

Ö, ö

Old Norse	English
öðru	other-things
öðrum	other, others
önnur	others

Œ, œ

Old Norse	English
œrin	mad
œskilegra	desirable

P, p

Old Norse	English
prests	priest

R, r

Old Norse	English
ráð	advice
ránfengi	robbery
reið	rode, was-riding
reiði	anger
rekkju	bed
riðit	riding, rode
riðu	rode
rjúfast	break

S, s

Word List (Old Norse to English)

Old Norse	English
sá	saw
sæng	bed
særðan	wounded
sæti	a-bench
sætti	reason
sagði	said, told
sama	same
samlags	union
segir	said
segja	be-said, say-to
seinat	0
seinna	later
sem	as, as-if, as-in, that, which, who, whom
sér	himself, his
settust	sat
sið	tradition, 0
síðan	afterwards, later
síðar	later
siðaskifti	conversion, the-conversion
siðr	a-custom
síðr	less
síðu-hallr	Sidu-Hall (name)
sigurðarsonar	Sigurdson (name)
sik	himself
sína	his, their
sinn	their
sinna	his, theirs
sinni	mind
síns	his
sínum	his
sitt	this
sjái	see
sjálfr	of-himself
skaða	damage
skal	shall
skatt	tribute
skipaði	directed
skömm	a-shame, shame
skuli	shall
skurðgoða	idols
skyldi	should
slíkum	such
sló	laid-out

Old Norse	English
smá	small
snúa	to-return
sœmdar	honour
sofa	sleep
sofi	sleep
sofnaðir	sleeping
son	son
sona	sons
sonar	son
sonr	son
sóttu	set-about
spakari	wiser
spámaðr	a-seer, the-Seer
spámann	the-Seer
spratt	sprang
spurði	asked
staðfesti	steadfast
stór	great
stundu	while
sumar	summer
sumarit	summer
sunnan	from-the-south
svá	so
svaraði	answered
svarar	answered
svarat	answered
svartklæddu	black-clothes
sverð	sword, swords
svörtum	black
sýndi	it-seemed
sýnina	this-sight
sýrlœkjarósi	Syrlaekjaros (place)

T, t

Old Norse	English
tíðindi	the-news, tidings
til	to, until
tilborðs	to-the-tables
tíma	time
tíu	ten
tjóa	that
tók	took
trúlega	truely
tunglskin	moonlight

Word List (Old Norse to English)

Old Norse	English

Þ, þ

Old Norse	English
þ.e	i.e.
þá	then, they, those
þær	there, they
þagði	silent
þangat	from-there
þangbrands	Thangbrand (name)
þann	that, that, then
þar	here, that, there
þarf	need
þat	it, that, the, the, the-matter
þau	than, there, they
þegar	once
þeim	them, they
þeir	they
þeira	of-them
þenna	these
þér	to-you, you
þess	this
þessa	this
þessi	this
þessu	this
þessum	this
þetta	this
þiðranda	Thidrandi (name)
þiðrandi	Thidrandi (name)
þik	you
þili	wall
þingi	the-assembly
þings	the-assembly
þinn	yours
þjóna	serve
þó	although, though
þórhall	Thorhall (name)
þórhalli	Thorhall (name)
þórhallr	Thorhall (name)
þórhalls	Thorhall's (name)
þótti	thought
þrældómi	slavery
þrisvar	three-times
þú	are-you, you
þváttá	Thvatta (place)
þváttár	Thvatta (place)
því	because, because-of, for, then, therefore, 0
þvílíkir	like
þykkir	think

U, u

Old Norse	English
um	about
unat	liked
undarliga	strange
undarligri	stranger
undi	on
undir	under
unni	loved
upp	up
urðu	came
uxa	ox

Ú, ú

Old Norse	English
út	out, outside

V, v

Old Norse	English
vænstr	handsome
væra	was
væri	the-home
vaknaði	woke
vald	power
vánir	the-hopes
var	was, were
varðist	defended
varu	was
váru	were
veðr	weather
veit	know
veizla	feast
veizlan	the-feast
veizlu	feast
vekti	awoke
vel	well
vera	be

Word List (Old Norse to English)

Old Norse	English
verða	be, become, come-to, happen
verit	been
verka	works
vetra	winters
vetrnóttum	winter-night
við	with
viðgerðar-mikit	widely-made-much
viðköstinn	the-wood-pile
vilda	will
vildi	willed
vilja	will
viljat	0
villuböndum	sins
vin	friend
vinátta	friendship
vinsælasti	endearing
vinum	friends
virði	values
virðist	seeming
vissi	knew
vissu	knew
vitat	known
vöktu	woke
völlinn	the-field

Y, y

yðr	you
yðrar	your, yours
yfir	over
yztr	outer

Word List (English to Old Norse)

Word List (English to Old Norse)

English	Old Norse
A, a	
a	í
a-bed-closet	hvílugólfinu
a-bench	sæti
about	um
accomplished	atgervismaðr
a-custom	siðr
admired	dáðust
advice	ráð
after	eftir
afterwards	eftir, síðan
age	aldr
Alftafjord (place)	álftafirði
all	alla, allan, allar, allir, alls, allt
a-long	langri
also	ok
although	þó
always	jafnan
a-man	maðr, manna
ambassadors	erindreka
am-I	ek
a-mound	haug
and	enn, og, ok
anger	reiði
another	annarri
answered	svaraði, svarar, svarat
anyone	nökkurr
approached	nálgast
are	er, eru
are-you	þú
as	at, enn, er, í, sem
a-seer	spámaðr
a-shame	skömm
as-if	sem
as-in	sem
ask	biðja
asked	bað, spurði
assisting	beina
at	á, at, í
at-the-door	dyra

English	Old Norse
autumn-feast	haustboði, haustboðinu
autumn-harvest	haustboðs
a-wise	fróðr
awoke	vekti
B, b	
back	aftr
bags	bagga
be	at, er, vera, verða
bears	berr
because	því
because-of	því
become	verða
bed	rekkju, sæng
bed-closet	hvílugólfi
been	verit
before	áðr, fyrir, fyrr, fyrri
beforehand	fyrir
be-killed	drepa
Berufjord (place)	berufirði
be-said	segja
best	bezt
better	betri
between	milli
black	svörtum
black-clothes	svartklæddu
bore	bar, borit
both	báðir, bæði
bravely	drengiliga
break	bregða, rjúfast
bright	ljósum
broken	brugðit
brought	fœrði
bulls	naut
burst-out-laughing	brosti
but	enn, heldr

C, c

Word List (English to Old Norse)

English	Old Norse	English	Old Norse
call	*kalla*	enemies	*óvinr*
called	*kallaðr*	enemies-of	*óvina*
came	*fór, kom, urðu*	enjoy	*njóta*
can	*kann*	enjoys	*njóti*
captive	*hertekinn*	eternal	*eilífrar*
carried	*borinn*	evening	*kveldit*
celebrated-time	*fagnaðartíma*	event	*atburðr*
child	*barn*	events	*atburð*
christian-message	*kristniboð*	every	*hvert*
clothes	*klæðum*	evil	*illu*
come	*koma*	explanation	*grein*
comes	*komi*		
come-to	*verða*		
coming	*komnir*		

F, f

English	Old Norse
far-sighted	*framsýnn*
father	*föður*
feast	*veizla, veizlu*
few	*fátt*
folk	*fólk*
follow	*furða, fylgja*
followers	*fylgjur, fylgt*
for	*fyrir, fyrr, því*
foretold	*boðaði*
for-long	*lengi*
found	*fann, fundu*
friend	*vin*
friends	*vinum*
friendship	*vinátta*
from	*af, frá, fram*
from-there	*þangat*
from-the-south	*sunnan*
frosty	*frostviðri*

compelled *nauðigr*
conversion *siðaskifti*
creature *kvikindi*
cried *kvað*
cruelty-full *grimdarfulla*
cursed *bölvuðu*

D, d

English	Old Norse
damage	*skaða*
damned	*fjandans*
daybreak	*lýsing*
deeds	*atgervi*
defended	*varðist*
desirable	*œskilegra*
died	*andaðist*
directed	*skipaði*
down	*niðr*
drawn-out	*brugðin*
dwelled	*dvaldist*

E, e

English	Old Norse
each	*hvert*
east	*austr*
eighteen	*átján*
eldest	*elzti*
endearing	*vinsælasti*
ended	*lokit*

G, g

English	Old Norse
gentle	*blíðr*
give	*gefi*
god	*guði*
goes	*gengr*
going	*ganga, gegna, gengit*
good	*búnu, góðra*
great	*mikil, stór*
greater	*meiri*
greatest	*mesta*

Word List (English to Old Norse)

English	*Old Norse*	English	*Old Norse*
guess	*get, geta*	I	*ek, mér*
guested	*gisti*	i.e.	*þ.e*
guests	*gestum*	Iceland (place)	*ísland, íslandi, íslands*
		idols	*skurðgoða*

H, h

		if	*ef*
had	*hafði, höfðu, lát, lét*	ill	*illt*
Hakon (name)	*hákonar*	in	*á, í*
Hall (name)	*halli, hallr*	inherited	*erfðar*
Hall's (name)	*halls*	inside	*inn*
hand	*hönd, höndum*	intended	*ætlat*
handsome	*vænstr*	into	*á*
happen	*verða*	invited	*bauð, býðr*
harm	*mein*	invited-men	*boðsmanna, boðsmenn*
has	*hefir*		
have	*á, hafa, hafi, hefði*	is	*er*
having	*hafa*	it	*á, þat*
he	*hann, hans, honum*	it-seemed	*sýndi*
health	*hagi*		
heard	*heyrði*

K, k

heathen	*heiðnum*		
heed	*gaum*	killed	*drepinn*
held	*haldit*	kindness	*blíðskap*
here	*hér, hingat, þar*	kinsmen	*frænda, frændr*
hills	*hóll*	knew	*vissi, vissu*
him	*hann, honum*	know	*veit*
himself	*sér, sik*	known	*vitat*
his	*hans, sér, sína, sinna, síns, sínum*

L, l

hissed	*hvessti*		
Hof (place)	*hofi*	laid	*lagðr*
hold	*halda*	laid-out	*sló*
home	*heim*	land	*land*
home-invitation	*heimboða, heimboði*	later	*seinna, síðan, síðar*
honour	*sœmdar*	laughing	*brosi, brosir*
Horgsland (place)	*hörgslandi*	lay	*lá, liggja*
horses	*hestum*	lead	*leiða*
how	*hverju, hversu*	less	*síðr*
humble	*mjúkr*	let	*láta*
		life	*líf*
		like	*þvílíkir*
		liked	*unat*
		little	*fátt, lítils, litlu*

I, i

		live	*búa*
		long	*löngum*

Word List (English to Old Norse)

English	*Old Norse*	English	*Old Norse*
longer	*lengr*	northern	*norrœnn*
look	*líta*	not	*eigi, ekki*
look-back	*eftirsjá*	now	*nú*
lot	*hlut*		
loved	*unni*		
lying	*liggja*		

M, m

O, o

English	*Old Norse*
mad	*œrin*
make	*gera*
make-like	*makligan*
making	*gera*
man	*maðr*
mankind	*mannkyns*
manned	*mannaðan*
many	*marga, margir, margr, mörgum*
may	*má, mun*
me	*mér*
meet	*móti*
mercifully	*miskunnaraugum*
mind	*sinni*
mine	*mín, míns, mínum*
mislike	*mislíki*
modest	*lítillátr*
moonlight	*tunglskin*
morning	*morgin, morgun*
most	*flest, flestir, hinn, mesta, mesti*
moving-day	*fardaga*
much	*mikil, mikit, mjök*
my	*mín, mitt*

English	*Old Norse*
of	*á, af, at, er, í*
of-all	*allra*
of-himself	*sjálfr*
often	*oft*
of-them	*þeira*
old	*gamlan*
omnipotent	*allsvaldandi*
on	*á, í, undi*
once	*þegar*
one	*einn, eitt*
or	*eðr*
or-that	*eðr*
other	*aðrar, aðrir, öðrum*
others	*aðrar, hitt, öðrum, önnur*
other-things	*öðru*
out	*út*
outer	*yztr*
outside	*út*
over	*yfir*
ox	*uxa*

N, n

P, p

English	*Old Norse*
need	*þarf*
news	*fréttum*
next	*næst*
night	*nótt*
nine	*níu*
no	*eigi, engan, engar, engi*
north	*norðan*

English	*Old Norse*
part	*hlutr*
passed	*leið*
people	*lýð, menn*
people's-travels	*mannaferðir*
person	*mann*
power	*vald*
praise	*lofa, lofi*
praised	*lofuðu*
preach	*boða*
prepare	*búa*
prepared	*búin*
prepares	*býr*
priest	*prests*
proclaims	*boðar*

Word List (English to Old Norse)

English	*Old Norse*	English	*Old Norse*
promised	*heitit*	sins	*villuböndum*
promising	*efniligastr*	slavery	*þrældómi*
publicly	*opinberliga*	sleep	*sofa, sofi*
		sleeping	*sofnaðir*
		small	*smá*
		so	*svá*
		some	*nökkurir, nökkurr*
		sometime	*nökkuru*
		son	*son, sonar, sonr*
		sons	*sona*
		speak	*kveða*
		spirits	*dísir*
		spoke	*mælti*
		sprang	*spratt*
		stayed	*haldit*
		steadfast	*staðfesti*
		stories	*frásagnir*
		stormy	*hvasst*
		strange	*undarliga*
		stranger	*undarligri*
		such	*slíkum*
		suggesting	*leggr*
		summer	*sumar, sumarit*
		summons	*kvatt*
		suppose	*ætla*
		sword	*sverð*
		swords	*sverð*
		Syrlaekjaros (place)	*sýrlœkjarósi*

R, r

English	*Old Norse*
raids	*áhlaupum*
reason	*sætti*
redeemed	*leysa*
rejected	*afhendir*
religion	*átrúnaði*
remarkable	*merkilegasti, merkilegt*
responds	*anzar*
riding	*riðit*
robbery	*ránfengi*
rode	*reið, riðit, riðu*

S, s

English	*Old Norse*
saddened	*ógleðja*
said	*mælti, sagði, segir*
same	*sama*
sat	*settust*
saw	*sá*
say	*mælir*
say-to	*segja*
scared	*hræddr*
see	*sjái*
seeming	*virðist*
serve	*þjóna*
set-about	*sóttu*
settled	*bjó, byggði*
settlement	*byggð*
shall	*gkal, mun, munit, munu, munut, skal, skuli*
shall-be	*munu*
shame	*skömm*
should	*mun, skyldi*
Sidu-Hall (name)	*síðu-hallr*
signs	*bendingum*
Sigurdson (name)	*sigurðarsonar*
silent	*þagði*

T, t

English	*Old Norse*
ten	*tíu*
than	*enn, þau*
Thangbrand (name)	*þangbrands*
that	*á, at, er, gera, haft, sem, þann, þar, þat, tjóa*
that-which	*er*
the	*at, hin, hinar, hinn, þat*
the-assembly	*þingi, þings*
the-conversion	*siðaskifti*
the-days-of	*dögum*
the-earl	*jarls*
the-farmer	*bóndi*

Word List (English to Old Norse)

English	Old Norse	English	Old Norse
the-feast	veizlan	to-have	lét
the-field	völlinn	to-help	hjálpa
the-home	væri	to-him	honum
the-hopes	vánir	told	fœrðir, sagði
the-house	heim	to-me	mér
their	sína, sinn	took	tók
theirs	sinna	too-late	of
the-land	lands	to-return	snúa
the-lands	landa	to-the-tables	tilborðs
them	þeim	to-you	þér
the-matter	þat	tradition	sið
the-men	mönnum	travel	fara
the-most	hinn, mest	travelled	fór
then	enn, þá, þann, því	tribute	skatt
the-news	tíðindi	truely	trúlega
the-people	menn		
there	þær, þar, þau		
therefore	því		
these	þenna		
the-Seer	spámaðr, spámann		
the-town	bœjar		
the-women	konurnar		
the-wood-pile	viðköstinn		
they	þá, þær, þau, þeim, þeir		
they-came	komust		
they-open	opnast		

U, u

English	Old Norse
under	undir
ungladness	ógleðjast
union	samlags
until	til
up	upp
usual	jafnan

English	Old Norse
Thidrandi (name)	þiðranda, þiðrandi
things	hluti, hlutir, hlutum
think	hygg, þykkir
this	sitt, þess, þessa, þessi, þessu, þessum, þetta
this-sight	sýnina
Thorhall (name)	þórhall, þórhalli, þórhallr
Thorhall's (name)	þórhalls
those	þá
though	þó
thought	hug, þótti
three-times	þrisvar
Thvatta (place)	þváttá, þváttár
tidings	tíðindi
time	tíma
to	á, at, í, til
to-break	boði

V, v

English	Old Norse
values	virði

W, w

English	Old Norse
wall	þili
war-takings	herfangs
was	er, væra, var, varu
was-named	hét
was-riding	reið
weather	veðr
well	vel
went	gekk, gengu
were	er, var, váru
what	er, hví
whatever	hverigir
when	enn, er

Word List (English to Old Norse)

English	Old Norse
where	*hvar*
whether	*hvárt*
which	*enn, er, sem*
while	*stundu*
white	*hvítum*
who	*er, sem*
wholly	*heilt*
whom	*sem*
why	*hví*
widely-made-much	*viðgerðar-mikit*
will	*hafa, vilda, vilja*
willed	*vildi*
window	*gluggr*
winter-night	*vetrnóttum*
winters	*vetra*
wiser	*spakari*
with	*með, við*
without	*laust*
woke	*vaknaði, vöktu*
women	*konur*
words	*orð*
works	*verka*
would	*mun, mundri, munu, myndi*
would-be	*mundu*
wounded	*særðan*

Y, y

you	*þér, þik, þú, yðr*
your	*yðrar*
yours	*þinn, yðrar*

The Tale of Thiðrandi and Thórhall (*Old Icelandic*)

Old Icelandic	Literal	English
1	**1**	**1**
Þórhallur hét maður norrænn.	Thorhall was-named a-man northern.	There was a nordic man named Thorhall.
Hann kom út til Íslands á dögum Hákonar jarls Sigurðarsonar.	He came out to Iceland in the-days-of Hakon the-earl Sigurdson.	He came out to Iceland in the days of earl Hakon Sigurdson.
Hann tók land í Sýrlækjarósi og bjó á Hörgslandi.	He took land in Syrlaekjaros and settled at Horgsland.	He took land in Syrlaekjaros and settled at Horgsland.
Þórhallur var fróður maður og mjög framsýnn og var kallaður Þórhallur spámaður.	Thorhall was a-wise man and much far-sighted and was called Thorhall the-Seer.	Thorhall was a wise man and very far-sighted, and he was called Thorhall the Seer
Þórhallur spámaður bjó þá á Hörgslandi er Síðu-Hallur bjó að Hofi í Álftafirði og var með þeim hin mesta vinátta.	Thorhall the-Seer settled then at Horgsland when Sidu-Hall settled at Hof in Alftafjord and was with them the most friendship.	Thorhall the Seer then settled at Horgsland when Sidu-Hall settled at Hof in Alftafjord and between them was the best friendship.
Gisti Hallur á Hörgslandi hvert sumar er hann reið til þings.	Guested Hall at Horgsland each summer as he rode to the-assembly.	Hall was a guest at Horgsland each summer as he ridden to the assembly.
Þórhallur fór og oft til heimboða austur þangað og var þar löngum.	Thorhall travelled also often to home-invitation east from-there and was there long.	Thorhall also travelled by invitation to the east and spent a long time there.
Sonur Halls hinn elsti hét Þiðrandi.	Son Hall's the eldest was-named Thidrandi.	Hall's eldest son was named Thidrand.
Hann var manna vænstur og efnilegastur.	He was a-man handsome and promising.	He was a handsom and promising man.
Unni Hallur honum mest allra sona sinna.	Loved Hall him the-most of-all sons his.	Hall loved him the most of all his sons.
Þiðrandi fór landa í milli þegar hann hafði aldur til.	Thidrandi travelled the-lands in between once he had age to.	Thidrand travelled between lands as soon as he was old enough.

The Tale of Thiðrandi and Thórhall (Old Icelandic)

Old Icelandic	Literal	English
Hann var hinn vinsælasti hvar sem hann kom því að hann var hinn mesti atgervimaður, lítillátur og blíður við hvert barn.	He was most endearing where that he came for that he was the most accomplished, modest and gentle with every child.	He was most endearing wherever he came, for he was the most accomplished but modest, and gentle with every man and child.
Það var eitt sumar að Hallur bauð Þórhalli vin sínum austur þangað þá er hann reið af þingi.	It was one summer that Hall invited Thorhall friend his east from-there then when he was-riding from the-assembly.	It happened one summer that Hall invited Thorhall his friend to the east when he was riding home from the assembly.
Þórhallur fór austur nokkuru síðar en Hallur og tók Hallur við honum sem jafnan með hinum mesta blíðskap.	Thorhall travelled east sometime later than Hall and took Hall with him as usual with the greatest kindness.	Thorhall travelled east sometime later than Hall, and Hall received him with with the greatest kindness as usual.
Dvaldist Þórhallur þar um sumarið og sagði Hallur að hann skyldi eigi fyrri fara heim en lokið væri haustboði.	Dwelled Thorhall there about summer and said Hall that he should not before travel home than ended the-home autumn-feast.	Thorhall dwelled there over the summer and Hall said that he should not travel home before the autumn feast had ended.
Það sumar kom Þiðrandi út í Berufirði.	That summer came Thidrandi out to Berufjord.	That summer Thidrand came out to Berufjord.
Þá var hann átján vetra.	Then was he eighteen winters.	Then he was 18 winters old.
Fór hann heim til föður síns.	Travelled he home to father his.	He travelled home to his father.
Dáðust menn þá enn mjög að honum sem oft áður og lofuðu atgervi hans en Þórhallur spámaður þagði jafnan þá er menn lofuðu hann mest.	Admired people then as much of him as often before and praised deeds his but Thorhall the-Seer silent always then when people praised him the-most.	People admired him as much as before and praised his deeds, but Thorhall the Seer was always silent when people praised him the most.
Þá spurði Hallur hví það sætti	Then asked Hall what the reason:	Then Hall asked what the reason was for this:
"því að mér þykir það merkilegt er þú mælir Þórhallur", segir hann.	"because that I think it remarkable that-which you say Thorhall", said he.	"because I think that whatever you say Thorhall is always remarkable to me", he said.
Þórhallur svaraði:	Thorhall answered:	Thorhall answered:

The Tale of Thiðrandi and Thórhall (Old Icelandic)

Old Icelandic	Literal	English
"Ekki gengur mér það til þess að mér mislíki nokkur hlutur við hann eða þig eða eg sjái síður en aðrir menn að hann er hinn merkilegasti maður heldur ber hitt til að margir verða til að lofa hann og hefir hann marga hluti til þess þó að hann virði sig lítils sjálfur.	"Not goes to-me that to this that I mislike some part with him or you or-that I see less than other people that he is the-most remarkable man but bears others to that many become until to praise him and has he many things to this although that he values himself little of-himself.	"It does not occur to me that I dislike anything about him or you, or that I see less than other men that he is the most remarkable man, but rather that many will praise him and he has many things to do with it, although he values himself little.
Kann það vera að hans njóti eigi lengi og mun þér þá ærin eftirsjá að um son þinn svo vel mannaðan þó að eigi lofi allir menn fyrir þér hans atgervi".	Can it be that he enjoys not for-long and should you then mad look-back that about son yours so well manned though that not praise all people for to-you his deeds".	It may be that he will not enjoy it for long, and then you will regret that your son is so well mannered, even though not all people praise you for his deeds".

2

En er á leið sumarið tók Þórhallur mjög að ógleðjast.	When was that passed summer took Thorhall much to ungladness.	When that summer was passed, Thorhall took much sadness.
Hallur spurði hví það sætti.	Hall asked what the reason.	Hall asked what the reason was.
Þórhallur svaraði:	Thorhall answered:	Thorhall answered:
"Illt hygg eg til haustboðs þessa er hér skal vera því að mér býður það fyrir að spámaður mun vera drepinn að þessi veislu".	"Ill think I to autumn-harvest this that here shall be for to me invited it for that a-seer shall be killed at this feast".	"I think evil of this autumn invitation which is to be here, for it offers me that a prophet will be killed at this feast".
"Þar kann eg að gera grein á", segir bóndi.	"Here can I that make explanation of", said the-farmer.	"I can explain that," said the farmer.
"Eg á uxa einn tíu vetra gamlan þann er eg kalla Spámann því að hann er spakari en flest naut önnur.	"I have ox one ten winters old that which I call The-Seer because that he is wiser than most bulls others.	"I have a ten-year-old ox, whom I call the Prophet, for he is wiser than most other bulls.

The Tale of Thiðrandi and Thórhall (Old Icelandic)

Old Icelandic	Literal	English
En hann skal drepa að haustboðinu og þarf þig þetta eigi að ógleðja því að eg ætla að þessi mín veisla sem aðrar skuli þér og öðrum vinum mínum verða til sæmdar".	But he shall be-killed at autumn-feast and need you this not be saddened because that I suppose that this my feast as others shall you and other friends mine be to honour".	But he will be killed at the autumn feast, and you need not be saddened because of this, for I think that this feast of mine, as well as others, will be an honour to you and to my other friends".
Þórhallur svarar:	Thorhall answered:	Thorhall answered:
"Eg fann þetta og eigi af því til að eg væri hræddur um mitt líf og boðar mér fyrir meiri tíðindi og undarlegri þau er eg mun að sinni eigi upp kveða".	"I found this and not of because to that I was scared about my life and proclaims to-me for greater tidings and stranger than is I may to mind not up speak".	"I found this not because I was afraid of my life, but because it proclaims to me more tidings and stranger ones that I have a mind not to speak up about".
Hallur mælti:	Hall said:	Hallur said:
"Þá er og ekki fyrir að bregða boði því".	"Then is and not for that break to-break therefore".	"Then there is no way to break the offer".
Þórhallur svarar:	Thorhall answered:	Þórhallur answered:
"Ekki mun það gera að mæla því að það mun fram ganga sem ætlað er".	"Not would that be that the-matter therefore that it should from going as intended be".	"It will not do in this matter because it will go as intended".
Veislan var búin að veturnóttum.	The-feast was prepared that winter-night.	The feast was prepared for the winter nights.
Kom þar fátt boðsmanna því að veður var hvasst og viðgerðarmikið.	Came there few invited-men because the weather was stormy and widely-made-much.	Few of the invited people came because the weather was stormy and difficult to travel in.
En er menn settust til borða um kveldið þá mælti Þórhallur:	When were the-people sat to the-tables about evening then spoke Thorhall:	When the people sat at the tables in the evening then Thorhall spoke:

The Tale of Thiðrandi and Thórhall (Old Icelandic)

Old Icelandic	Literal	English
"Biðja vildi eg að menn hefðu ráð mín um það að engi maður komi hér út á þessi nótt því að mikil mein munu hér á liggja ef af þessu er brugðið og hverigir hlutir sem verða í bendingum gefi menn eigi gaum að því, að illu mun furða ef nokkur ansar til".	"Ask will I that people have advice mine about it that no man comes here outside on this night for that much harm shall here to lay if of this is broken and whatever things which happen as signs give people not heed to for, that evil shall follow if anyone responds to".	"I wish to ask that people hear my advice that no man goes outside on this night, for there shall be much harm if this is broken and whatever things people might see as signs are to be given no heed to, for evil shall follow if anyone answers".
Hallur bað menn halda orð Þórhalls	Hall asked people hold words Thorhall's:	Hall asked people to hold to Thorhall's words:
"því að þau rjúfast ekki", segir hann,	"because that they break not", said he,	"because they will not break", he said,
"og er um heilt best að búa".	"and is about wholly best to prepare".	"and it will be best to be wholly prepared".
Þiðrandi gekk um beina.	Thidrandi went about assisting.	Thidrand went about assisting.
Var hann í því sem öðru mjúkur og lítillátur.	Was he as then as-in other-things humble and modest.	He was as in other things humble and modest.
En er menn gengu að sofa þá skipaði Þiðrandi gestum í sæng sína en hann sló sér niður í seti ystur við þili.	But when people went to sleep then directed Thidrandi guests to bed his but he laid-out himself down on a-bench outer with wall.	But when people went to sleep Thidrand directed guests to his bed and he laid himself down on a bench at the outermost wall.
En er flestir menn voru sofnaðir þá var kvatt dura og lét engi maður sem vissi.	When that most people were sleeping then was summons at-the-door and had no man as-if knew.	When most people were asleep there was a summons at the door, but no man acted as if they knew of it.
Fór svo þrisvar.	Came so three-times.	It came three times.
Þá spratt Þiðrandi upp og mælti:	Then sprang Thidrandi up and spoke:	Then Thidrand sprang up and spoke:
"Þetta er skömm mikil er menn láta hér allir sem sofi og munu boðsmenn komnir".	"This is a-shame great that people let here all who sleep and shall-be invited-men coming".	"This is a great shame that the people here are asleep and these must be guests coming".
Hann tók sverð í hönd sér og gekk út.	He took sword in hand his and went out.	He took his sword in his hand and went out.
Hann sá engan mann.	He saw no person.	He saw no person.

The Tale of Thiðrandi and Thórhall (Old Icelandic)

Old Icelandic	Literal	English
Honum kom þá það í hug að nokkurir boðsmenn mundu hafa riðið fyrir heim til bæjarins og riðið síðan aftur í móti þeim er seinna riðu.	To-him came then that a thought that some invited-men would have rode for the-house to the-town and rode afterwards back to meet them that later rode.	A thought came to him that some guests would have ridden to the house and then back to the town to meet those who had ridden behind them arriving later.
Hann gekk þá undir viðköstinn og heyrði að riðið var norðan á völlinn.	He went then under the-wood-pile and heard that riding was north into the-field.	He walked under the wood pile and heard the sound of riding coming from the north into the field.
Hann sá að það voru konur níu og voru allar í svörtum klæðum og höfðu brugðin sverð í höndum.	He saw that it was women nine and were all in black clothes and had drawn-out swords in hand.	He saw that there were nine women and they were all in black clothes and had drawn swords in their hands.
Hann heyrði og að riðið var sunnan á völlinn.	He heard also that riding was from-the-south into the-field.	He also heard the sound of riding coming from the south into the field.
Þar voru og níu konur, allar í ljósum klæðum og á hvítum hestum.	There were also nine women, all in bright clothes and on white horses.	There were also nine women, all in bright clothes and on white horses.
Þá vildi Þiðrandi snúa inn og segja mönnum sýnina en þá bar að konurnar fyrr, hinar svartklæddu, og sóttu að honum en hann varðist drengilega.	Then willed Thidrandi to-return inside and say-to the-men this-sight but then bore to the-women before, the black-clothes, and set-about to him and he defended bravely.	Then Thidrand wished to return inside and tell the men of what he had seen, but then the women in the black clothes came upon him first and set about him, and he defended himself bravely.

3

Old Icelandic	Literal	English
En langri stundu síðar vaknaði Þórhallur og spurði hvort Þiðrandi vekti og var honum eigi svarað.	Then a-long while later woke Thorhall and asked whether Thidrandi awoke and was he not answered.	A long while later Thorhall woke and asked whether Thidrand was awake but he was not answered.
Þórhallur kvað þá mundu ofseinað.	Thorhall cried then would-be too-late.	Thorhall cried out that it would be too late.
Var þá út gengið.	Were they out going.	They went outside.

The Tale of Thiðrandi and Thórhall (Old Icelandic)

Old Icelandic	Literal	English
Var á tunglskin og frostviðri.	Was it moonlight and frosty.	It was moonlight and frosty.
Þeir fundu Þiðranda liggja særðan og var hann borinn inn.	They found Thidrandi lying wounded and was he carried inside.	They found Thidrand lying wounded and was he carried inside.
Og er menn höfðu orð við hann sagði hann þetta allt sem fyrir hann hafði borið.	And when people had words with him told he this all that before he had bore.	And when the people had gotten word from him, he told them all that had happened before.
Hann andaðist þann sama morgun í lýsing og var lagður í haug að heiðnum sið.	He died that same morning at daybreak and was laid in a-mound as heathen tradition.	He died that same morning at daybreak and was laid in a mound as in the heathen tradition.
Síðan var haldið fréttum til um mannaferðir og vissu menn ekki vonir óvina Þiðranda.	Later was held news of about people's-travels and knew people not the-hopes enemies-of Thidrandi.	Later there was news of peoples' travels and people did not know the hopes of Thidrand's enemies.
Hallur spurði Þórhall hverju gegna mundi um þenna undarlega atburð.	Hall asked Thorhall how going would about these strange events.	Hall asked Thorhall how these strange events would turn out.
Þórhallur svarar:	Thorhall answered:	Thorhall answered:
"Það veit eg eigi en geta má eg til að þetta hafi engar konur verið aðrar en fylgjur yðrar frænda.	"That know I not but guess may I to that this have no women been other than followers your kinsmen.	"That I do not know, but I guess that these women can only have been followers of your kinsmen.
Get eg að hér eftir komi siðaskipti og mun því næst koma siður betri hingað til lands.	Guess I that here after comes conversion and should therefore next come a-custom better here to the-land.	I guess that there shall come a conversion, and there will be a better custom here to the land.
Ætla eg þær dísir yðrar er fylgt hafa þessum átrúnaði munu hafa vitað fyrir siðaskiptið og fyrir það að þér munuð verða þeim afhendir frændur.	Suppose I there spirits yours were followers having this religion would have known beforehand the-conversion and before it that you shall come-to them rejected kinsmen.	I suppose that these spirits of you who have followed the old faith would have known beforehand about this conversion, and that they would be rejected by your kinsmen.
Nú munu þær eigi hafa því unað að hafa engan skatt af yður áður og munu þær þetta hafa í sinn hlut.	Now shall they not have therefore liked to have no tribute from you before and would there that have in their lot.	Now they will not have liked to have had no tribute from you before and they would therefore have their lot.

133

The Tale of Thiðrandi and Thórhall (Old Icelandic)

Old Icelandic	Literal	English
En hinar betri dísir mundu vilja hjálpa honum og komust eigi við að svo búnu.	But the better spirits would will to-help him and they-came not with to so good.	But the better spirits would have wished to help him, but they did not arrive in time.
Nú munuð þér frændur þeirra njóta er þann munuð hafa er þær boða fyrir og fylgja".	Now shall you kinsmen of-them enjoy which then shall have what they preach for and follow".	Now your kinsmen shall enjoy the help of them by following what they preach for".
Nú boðaði þessi atburður fyrir sem Þórhallur sagði og margir hlutir þvílíkir þann fagnaðartíma sem eftir kom, að allsvaldandi guð virtist að líta miskunnaraugum á þann lýð er Ísland byggði og leysa það fólk fyrir sína erindreka af löngum fjandans þrældómi og leiða síðan til samlags eilífrar erfðar sinna æskilegra sona sem hann hefir fyrirheitið alla þá er honum vilja trúlega þjóna með staðfesti góðra verka.	Now foretold this event for which Thorhall said and many things like that celebrated-time which afterwards came, to omnipotent god seeming to look mercifully to that people of Iceland settled and redeemed that folk for their ambassadors of long damned slavery and lead afterwards to union eternal inherited his desirable sons whom he has fore-promised all those who him will truely serve with steadfast good works.	Now this event was foretold which Thorhall had said many things about, the celebrated time which came afterwards, an omnipotent god seeing and looking mercifully to the people that settled Iceland, redeeming the people from their ambassadors of long and damned slavery, leading afterwards to an eternal union, inherited by his desirable sons, that he has promised to all those who will truly serve him with steadfast good works.
Svo og eigi síður sýndi óvinur alls mannkyns opinberlega í slíkum hlutum og mörgum öðrum þeim er í frásagnir eru færðir hversu nauðigur hann lét laust sitt ránfengi og þann lýð er hann hafði áður allan tíma haldið hertekinn í villuböndum sinna bölvaðra skurðgoða þá er hann hvessti með slíkum áhlaupum sína grimmdarfulla reiði á þeim sem hann hafði vald yfir sem hann vissi nálgast sína skömm og maklegan skaða síns herfangs.	So and no less it-seemed enemies all mankind publicly in such things and many others they are of stories are told how compelled he to-have without this robbery and that people that he had before all time stayed captive of sins theirs cursed idols then when he hissed with such raids his cruelty-full anger at them which he had power over which he knew approached their shame and make-like damage his war-takings.	So and it seemed no less that the enemies of all mankind publicly and in such things and many others, of which there are stories told of how they were compelled to abandon robbery, and the people that had before remained captive of the sins of their cursed idols when they hissed with such brutality and cruelty-full anger at those which they had power over, of which they knew they approached their shame, and the damage of their war-takings.
En Halli þótti svo mikið lát Þiðranda sonar síns að hann undi eigi lengur að búa að Hofi.	But Hall thought so much had Thidrandi son his that he on not longer to live at Hof.	But Halli thought so much of his son Thidrand's death that he could no longer live at Hof.

The Tale of Thiðrandi and Thórhall (Old Icelandic)

Old Icelandic	Literal	English
Færði hann þá byggð sína til Þvottár.	Brought he then settlement his to Thvatta.	He then moved his settlement to Thvatta.
Það var einn tíma að Þvottá þá er Þórhallur spámaður var þar að heimboði með Halli.	It was one time at Thvatta then that Thorhall the-Seer was there at home-invitation with Hall.	There was a time at Thvatta when Thorhall the Seer was invited to stay with Hall.
Hallur lá í hvílugólfi og Þórhallur í annarri rekkju en gluggur var á hvílugólfinu.	Hall lay in bed-closet and Thorhall in another bed which window was on a-bed-closet.	Hall lay in a bed-closet and Thorhall in another bed-closet which had a window.
Og einn morgun er þeir vöktu báðir þá brosti Þórhallur.	And one morning when they woke both then burst-out-laughing Thorhall.	And one morning they both woke and then Thorhall burst out laughing.
Hallur mælti:	Hall spoke:	Hall spoke:
"Hví brosir þú nú?"	"Why laughing are-you now?"	"Why are you laughing now?"
Þórhallur svarar:	Thorhall answered:	Thorhall answered:
"Að því brosi eg að margur hóll opnast og hvert kvikvendi býr sinn bagga, bæði smá og stór, og gera fardaga".	"That because-of laughing am-I that many hills they-open and every creature prepares their bags, both small and great, and making moving-day".	"I am laughing because many hills are opening, and every creature prepares their bags, both small and great, and does their moving-day".
Og litlu síðar urðu þau tíðindi sem nú skal frá segja.	And little later came there the-news that now shall from be-said.	And a little while later there came the news that shall now be said from.

Word List (Old Icelandic to English)

Old Icelandic	English
A, a	
að	as, at, be, of, that, the, to
aðrar	other, others
aðrir	other
af	from, from, of, of
afhendir	rejected
aftur	back
aldur	age
alla	all
allan	all
allar	all
allir	all, all
allra	of-all
alls	all
allsvaldandi	omnipotent
allt	all
andaðist	died
annarri	another
ansar	responds
atburð	events
atburður	event
atgervi	deeds, deeds
atgervimaður	accomplished
austur	east, east
Á, á	
á	at, have, in, into, it, of, on, that, to
áður	before
áhlaupum	raids
álftafirði	Alftafjord (place)
átján	eighteen
átrúnaði	religion
Æ, æ	
ærin	mad
æskilegra	desirable
ætla	suppose
ætlað	intended
B, b	
bað	asked
báðir	both
bæði	both
bæjarins	the-town
bagga	bags
bar	bore
barn	child
bauð	invited
beina	assisting
bendingum	signs
ber	bears
berufirði	Berufjord (place)
best	best
betri	better
biðja	ask
bjó	settled
blíðskap	kindness
blíður	gentle
boða	preach
boðaði	foretold
boðar	proclaims
boði	to-break
boðsmanna	invited-men
boðsmenn	invited-men
bölvaðra	cursed
bóndi	the-farmer
borða	the-tables
borið	bore
borinn	carried
bregða	break
brosi	laughing
brosir	laughing
brosti	burst-out-laughing
brugðið	broken
brugðin	drawn-out
búa	live, prepare
búin	prepared
búnu	good
býður	invited

Word List (Old Icelandic to English)

Old Icelandic	English
byggð	settlement
byggði	settled
býr	prepares

D, d

dáðust	admired
dísir	spirits
dögum	the-days-of
drengilega	bravely
drepa	be-killed
drepinn	killed
dura	at-the-door
dvaldist	dwelled

E, e

eða	or, or-that
ef	if
efnilegastur	promising
eftir	after, afterwards
eftirsjá	look-back
eg	am-I, I
eigi	no, not
eilífrar	eternal
einn	one
eitt	one
ekki	not
elsti	eldest
en	and, but, than, then, when, which
engan	no
engar	no
engi	no
enn	as
er	are, as, be, is, of, that, that-which, was, were, what, when, which, who
erfðar	inherited
erindreka	ambassadors
eru	are

F, f

Old Icelandic	English
færði	brought
færðir	told
fagnaðartíma	celebrated-time
fann	found
fara	travel
fardaga	moving-day
fátt	few
fjandans	damned
flest	most
flestir	most
föður	father
fólk	folk
fór	came, travelled
frá	from
frænda	kinsmen
frændur	kinsmen
fram	from
framsýnn	far-sighted
frásagnir	stories
fréttum	news
fróður	a-wise
frostviðri	frosty
fundu	found
furða	follow
fylgja	follow
fylgjur	followers
fylgt	followers
fyrir	before, beforehand, for
fyrirheitið	fore-promised
fyrr	before
fyrri	before

G, g

gamlan	old
ganga	going
gaum	heed
gefi	give
gegna	going
gekk	went
gengið	going
gengu	went
gengur	goes

Word List (Old Icelandic to English)

Old Icelandic	English
gera	be, make, making
gestum	guests
get	guess
geta	guess
gisti	guested
gluggur	window
góðra	good
grein	explanation
grimmdarfulla	cruelty-full
guð	god

H, h

Old Icelandic	English
hafa	have, having
hafði	had
hafi	have
hákonar	Hakon (name)
halda	hold
haldið	held, stayed
halli	Hall (name)
halls	Hall's (name)
hallur	Hall (name)
hann	he, him
hans	he, his
haug	a-mound
haustboði	autumn-feast
haustboðinu	autumn-feast
haustboðs	autumn-harvest
hefðu	have
hefir	has
heiðnum	heathen
heilt	wholly
heim	home, the-house
heimboða	home-invitation
heimboði	home-invitation
heldur	but
hér	here
herfangs	war-takings
hertekinn	captive
hestum	horses
hét	was-named
heyrði	heard
hin	the
hinar	the
hingað	here
hinn	most, the, the-most
hinum	the
hitt	others
hjálpa	to-help
hlut	lot
hluti	things
hlutir	things
hlutum	things
hlutur	part
höfðu	had
hofi	Hof (place)
hóll	hills
hönd	hand
höndum	hand
honum	he, him, to-him
hörgslandi	Horgsland (place)
hræddur	scared
hug	thought
hvar	where
hvasst	stormy
hverigir	whatever
hverju	how
hversu	how
hvert	each, every
hvessti	hissed
hví	what, why
hvílugólfi	bed-closet
hvílugólfinu	a-bed-closet
hvítum	white
hvort	whether
hygg	think

I, i

Old Icelandic	English
illt	ill
illu	evil
inn	inside

Í, í

Old Icelandic	English
í	a, as, at, in, of, on, to

Word List (Old Icelandic to English)

Old Icelandic	English
ísland	Iceland (place)
íslands	Iceland (place)

J, j

jafnan	always, usual
jarls	the-earl

K, k

kalla	call
kallaður	called
kann	can
klæðum	clothes
kom	came
koma	come
komi	comes
komnir	coming
komust	they-came
konur	women
konurnar	the-women
kvað	cried
kvatt	summons
kveða	speak
kveldið	evening
kvikvendi	creature

L, l

lá	lay
lagður	laid
land	land
landa	the-lands
lands	the-land
langri	a-long
lát	had
láta	let
laust	without
leið	passed
leiða	lead
lengi	for-long
lengur	longer
lét	had, to-have
leysa	redeemed
líf	life
liggja	lay, lying
líta	look
lítillátur	modest
lítils	little
litlu	little
ljósum	bright
lofa	praise
lofi	praise
lofuðu	praised
lokið	ended
löngum	long
lýð	people
lýsing	daybreak

M, m

má	may
maður	a-man, man
mæla	the-matter
mælir	say
mælti	said, spoke, spoke
maklegan	make-like
mann	person
manna	a-man
mannaðan	manned
mannaferðir	people's-travels
mannkyns	mankind
marga	many
margir	many
margur	many
með	with
mein	harm
meiri	greater
menn	people, the-people
mér	I, me, to-me
merkilegasti	remarkable
merkilegt	remarkable
mest	the-most
mesta	greatest, most
mesti	most
mikið	much
mikil	great, much
milli	between

Word List (Old Icelandic to English)

Old Icelandic	English
mín	mine, my
mínum	mine
miskunnaraugum	mercifully
mislíki	mislike
mitt	my
mjög	much
mjúkur	humble
mönnum	the-men
mörgum	many
morgun	morning
móti	meet
mun	may, shall, should, would
mundi	would
mundu	would, would-be
munu	shall, shall-be, would
munuð	shall

N, n

Old Icelandic	English
næst	next
nálgast	approached
nauðigur	compelled
naut	bulls
niður	down
níu	nine
njóta	enjoy
njóti	enjoys
nokkur	anyone, some
nokkurir	some
nokkuru	sometime
norðan	north
norrænn	northern
nótt	night
nú	now

O, o

Old Icelandic	English
ofseinað	too-late
oft	often
og	also, and
opinberlega	publicly
opnast	they-open
orð	words

Ó, ó

Old Icelandic	English
ógleðja	saddened
ógleðjast	ungladness
óvina	enemies-of
óvinur	enemies

Ö, ö

Old Icelandic	English
öðru	other-things
öðrum	other, others
önnur	others

R, r

Old Icelandic	English
ráð	advice
ránfengi	robbery
reið	rode, was-riding
reiði	anger
rekkju	bed
riðið	riding, rode
riðu	rode
rjúfast	break

S, s

Old Icelandic	English
sá	saw
sæmdar	honour
sæng	bed
særðan	wounded
sætti	reason
sagði	said, said, told
sama	same
samlags	union
segir	said
segja	be-said, say-to
seinna	later

Word List (Old Icelandic to English)

Old Icelandic	English
sem	as, as-if, as-in, that, which, who, whom
sér	himself, his
seti	a-bench
settust	sat
sið	tradition
síðan	afterwards, later
síðar	later
siðaskipti	conversion
siðaskiptið	the-conversion
síðu-hallur	Sidu-Hall (name)
siður	a-custom
síður	less
sig	himself
sigurðarsonar	Sigurdson (name)
sína	his, their
sinn	their
sinna	his, theirs
sinni	mind
síns	his
sínum	his
sitt	this
sjái	see
sjálfur	of-himself
skaða	damage
skal	shall
skatt	tribute
skipaði	directed
skömm	a-shame, shame
skuli	shall
skurðgoða	idols
skyldi	should
slíkum	such
sló	laid-out
smá	small
snúa	to-return
sofa	sleep
sofi	sleep
sofnaðir	sleeping
son	son
sona	sons
sonar	son
sonur	son
sóttu	set-about
spakari	wiser
spámaður	a-seer, the-Seer
spámann	the-Seer
spratt	sprang
spurði	asked
staðfesti	steadfast
stór	great
stundu	while
sumar	summer
sumarið	summer
sunnan	from-the-south
svarað	answered
svaraði	answered
svarar	answered
svartklæddu	black-clothes
sverð	sword, swords
svo	so
svörtum	black
sýndi	it-seemed
sýnina	this-sight
sýrlækjarósi	Syrlaekjaros (place)

T, t

Old Icelandic	English
tíðindi	the-news, tidings
til	of, to, until
tíma	time
tíu	ten
tók	took
trúlega	truely
tunglskin	moonlight

Þ, þ

Old Icelandic	English
þá	then, they, those
það	it, that, the
þær	there, they
þagði	silent
þangað	from-there
þann	that, that, then
þar	here, there
þarf	need
þau	than, there, they
þegar	once
þeim	them, they
þeir	they

Word List (Old Icelandic to English)

Old Icelandic	English
þeirra	of-them
þenna	these
þér	to-you, you
þess	this
þessa	this
þessi	this
þessu	this
þessum	this
þetta	that, this
þiðranda	Thidrandi (name)
þiðrandi	Thidrandi (name)
þig	you
þili	wall
þingi	the-assembly
þings	the-assembly
þinn	yours
þjóna	serve
þó	although, though
þórhall	Thorhall (name)
þórhalli	Thorhall (name)
þórhalls	Thorhall's (name)
þórhallur	Thorhall (name)
þótti	thought
þrældómi	slavery
þrisvar	three-times
þú	are-you, you
því	because, because-of, for, then, therefore
þvílíkir	like
þvottá	Thvatta (place)
þvottár	Thvatta (place)
þykir	think

U, u

Old Icelandic	English
um	about
unað	liked
undarlega	strange
undarlegri	stranger
undi	on
undir	under
unni	loved
upp	up
urðu	came
uxa	ox

Ú, ú

Old Icelandic	English
út	out, outside

V, v

Old Icelandic	English
vænstur	handsome
væri	the-home, was
vaknaði	woke
vald	power
var	was, were
varðist	defended
veður	weather
veisla	feast
veislan	the-feast
veislu	feast
veit	know
vekti	awoke
vel	well
vera	be
verða	be, become, come-to, happen
verið	been
verka	works
vetra	winters
veturnóttum	winter-night
við	with
viðgerðarmikið	widely-made-much
viðköstinn	the-wood-pile
vildi	will, willed
vilja	will
villuböndum	sins
vin	friend
vinátta	friendship
vinsælasti	endearing
vinum	friends
virði	values
virtist	seeming
vissi	knew
vissu	knew
vitað	known
vöktu	woke
völlinn	the-field

Word List (Old Icelandic to English)

Old Icelandic	English
vonir	the-hopes
voru	was, were

Y, y

yðrar	your, yours
yður	you
yfir	over
ystur	outer

Word List (English to Old Icelandic)

Word List (English to Old Icelandic)

English	*Old Icelandic*

A, a

a	*í*
a-bed-closet	*hvílugólfinu*
a-bench	*seti*
about	*um*
accomplished	*atgervimaður*
a-custom	*siður*
admired	*dáðust*
advice	*ráð*
after	*eftir*
afterwards	*eftir, síðan*
age	*aldur*
Alftafjord (place)	*álftafirði*
all	*alla, allan, allar, allir, alls, allt*
a-long	*langri*
also	*og*
although	*þó*
always	*jafnan*
a-man	*maður, manna*
ambassadors	*erindreka*
am-I	*eg*
a-mound	*haug*
and	*en, og*
anger	*reiði*
another	*annarri*
answered	*svarað, svaraði, svarar*
anyone	*nokkur*
approached	*nálgast*
are	*er, eru*
are-you	*þú*
as	*að, enn, er, í, sem*
a-seer	*spámaður*
a-shame	*skömm*
as-if	*sem*
as-in	*sem*
ask	*biðja*
asked	*bað, spurði*
assisting	*beina*
at	*á, að, í*
at-the-door	*dura*

English	*Old Icelandic*
autumn-feast	*haustboði, haustboðinu*
autumn-harvest	*haustboðs*
a-wise	*fróður*
awoke	*vekti*

B, b

back	*aftur*
bags	*bagga*
be	*að, er, gera, vera, verða*
bears	*ber*
because	*því*
because-of	*því*
become	*verða*
bed	*rekkju, sæng*
bed-closet	*hvílugólfi*
been	*verið*
before	*áður, fyrir, fyrr, fyrri*
beforehand	*fyrir*
be-killed	*drepa*
Berufjord (place)	*berufirði*
be-said	*segja*
best	*best*
better	*betri*
between	*milli*
black	*svörtum*
black-clothes	*svartklæddu*
bore	*bar, borið*
both	*báðir, bæði*
bravely	*drengilega*
break	*bregða, rjúfast*
bright	*ljósum*
broken	*brugðið*
brought	*færði*
bulls	*naut*
burst-out-laughing	*brosti*
but	*en, heldur*

C, c

144

Word List (English to Old Icelandic)

English	*Old Icelandic*	English	*Old Icelandic*
call	*kalla*	enjoy	*njóta*
called	*kallaður*	enjoys	*njóti*
came	*fór, kom, urðu*	eternal	*eilífrar*
can	*kann*	evening	*kveldið*
captive	*hertekinn*	event	*atburður*
carried	*borinn*	events	*atburð*
celebrated-time	*fagnaðartíma*	every	*hvert*
child	*barn*	evil	*illu*
clothes	*klæðum*	explanation	*grein*
come	*koma*		
comes	*komi*		
come-to	*verða*		
coming	*komnir*		
compelled	*nauðigur*		
conversion	*siðaskipti*		
creature	*kvikvendi*		
cried	*kvað*		
cruelty-full	*grimmdarfulla*		
cursed	*bölvaðra*		

F, f

English	*Old Icelandic*
far-sighted	*framsýnn*
father	*föður*
feast	*veisla, veislu*
few	*fátt*
folk	*fólk*
follow	*furða, fylgja*
followers	*fylgjur, fylgt*
for	*fyrir, því*
fore-promised	*fyrirheitið*
foretold	*boðaði*
for-long	*lengi*
found	*fann, fundu*
friend	*vin*
friends	*vinum*
friendship	*vinátta*
from	*af, frá, fram*
from-there	*þangað*
from-the-south	*sunnan*
frosty	*frostviðri*

D, d

English	*Old Icelandic*
damage	*skaða*
damned	*fjandans*
daybreak	*lýsing*
deeds	*atgervi*
defended	*varðist*
desirable	*æskilegra*
died	*andaðist*
directed	*skipaði*
down	*niður*
drawn-out	*brugðin*
dwelled	*dvaldist*

E, e

English	*Old Icelandic*
each	*hvert*
east	*austur*
eighteen	*átján*
eldest	*elsti*
endearing	*vinsælasti*
ended	*lokið*
enemies	*óvinur*
enemies-of	*óvina*

G, g

English	*Old Icelandic*
gentle	*blíður*
give	*gefi*
god	*guð*
goes	*gengur*
going	*ganga, gegna, gengið*
good	*búnu, góðra*
great	*mikil, stór*
greater	*meiri*
greatest	*mesta*
guess	*get, geta*

Word List (English to Old Icelandic)

English	*Old Icelandic*	English	*Old Icelandic*
guested	*gisti*	Iceland (place)	*Ísland, Íslands*
guests	*gestum*	idols	*skurðgoða*
		if	*ef*
		ill	*illt*
		in	*á, í*
		inherited	*erfðar*
		inside	*inn*
		intended	*ætlað*
		into	*á*
		invited	*bauð, býður*
		invited-men	*boðsmanna, boðsmenn*
		is	*er*
		it	*á, það*
		it-seemed	*sýndi*

H, h

English	*Old Icelandic*
had	*hafði, höfðu, lát, lét*
Hakon (name)	*hákonar*
Hall (name)	*halli, hallur*
Hall's (name)	*halls*
hand	*hönd, höndum*
handsome	*vænstur*
happen	*verða*
harm	*mein*
has	*hefir*
have	*á, hafa, hafi, hefðu*
having	*hafa*
he	*hann, hans, honum*
heard	*heyrði*
heathen	*heiðnum*
heed	*gaum*
held	*haldið*
here	*hér, hingað, þar*
hills	*hóll*
him	*hann, honum*
himself	*sér, sig*
his	*hans, sér, sína, sinna, síns, sínum*
hissed	*hvessti*
Hof (place)	*hofi*
hold	*halda*
home	*heim*
home-invitation	*heimboða, heimboði*
honour	*sæmdar*
Horgsland (place)	*hörgslandi*
horses	*hestum*
how	*hverju, hversu*
humble	*mjúkur*

I, i

English	*Old Icelandic*
I	*eg, mér*

K, k

English	*Old Icelandic*
killed	*drepinn*
kindness	*blíðskap*
kinsmen	*frænda, frændur*
knew	*vissi, vissu*
know	*veit*
known	*vitað*

L, l

English	*Old Icelandic*
laid	*lagður*
laid-out	*sló*
land	*land*
later	*seinna, síðan, síðar*
laughing	*brosi, brosir*
lay	*lá, liggja*
lead	*leiða*
less	*síður*
let	*láta*
life	*líf*
like	*þvílíkir*
liked	*unað*
little	*lítils, litlu*
live	*búa*
long	*löngum*
longer	*lengur*
look	*líta*

Word List (English to Old Icelandic)

English	*Old Icelandic*
look-back	*eftirsjá*
lot	*hlut*
loved	*unni*
lying	*liggja*

M, m

English	*Old Icelandic*
mad	*ærin*
make	*gera*
make-like	*maklegan*
making	*gera*
man	*maður*
mankind	*mannkyns*
manned	*mannaðan*
many	*marga, margir, margur, mörgum*
may	*má, mun*
me	*mér*
meet	*móti*
mercifully	*miskunnaraugum*
mind	*sinni*
mine	*mín, mínum*
mislike	*mislíki*
modest	*lítillátur*
moonlight	*tunglskin*
morning	*morgun*
most	*flest, flestir, hinn, mesta, mesti*
moving-day	*fardaga*
much	*mikið, mikil, mjög*
my	*mín, mitt*

N, n

English	*Old Icelandic*
need	*þarf*
news	*fréttum*
next	*næst*
night	*nótt*
nine	*níu*
no	*eigi, engan, engar, engi*
north	*norðan*
northern	*norrænn*
not	*eigi, ekki*
now	*nú*

O, o

English	*Old Icelandic*
of	*á, að, af, er, í, til*
of-all	*allra*
of-himself	*sjálfur*
often	*oft*
of-them	*þeirra*
old	*gamlan*
omnipotent	*allsvaldandi*
on	*á, í, undi*
once	*þegar*
one	*einn, eitt*
or	*eða*
or-that	*eða*
other	*aðrar, aðrir, öðrum*
others	*aðrar, hitt, öðrum, önnur*
other-things	*öðru*
out	*út*
outer	*ystur*
outside	*út*
over	*yfir*
ox	*uxa*

P, p

English	*Old Icelandic*
part	*hlutur*
passed	*leið*
people	*lýð, menn*
people's-travels	*mannaferðir*
person	*mann*
power	*vald*
praise	*lofa, lofi*
praised	*lofuðu*
preach	*boða*
prepare	*búa*
prepared	*búin*
prepares	*býr*
proclaims	*boðar*
promising	*efnilegastur*
publicly	*opinberlega*

Word List (English to Old Icelandic)

English	Old Icelandic

R, r

raids	áhlaupum
reason	sætti
redeemed	leysa
rejected	afhendir
religion	átrúnaði
remarkable	merkilegasti, merkilegt
responds	ansar
riding	riðið
robbery	ránfengi
rode	reið, riðið, riðu

S, s

saddened	ógleðja
said	mælti, sagði, segir
same	sama
sat	settust
saw	sá
say	mælir
say-to	segja
scared	hræddur
see	sjái
seeming	virtist
serve	þjóna
set-about	sóttu
settled	bjó, byggði
settlement	byggð
shall	mun, munu, munuð, skal, skuli
shall-be	munu
shame	skömm
should	mun, skyldi
Sidu-Hall (name)	síðu-hallur
signs	bendingum
Sigurdson (name)	sigurðarsonar
silent	þagði
sins	villuböndum
slavery	þrældómi
sleep	sofa, sofi
sleeping	sofnaðir
small	smá

English	Old Icelandic
so	svo
some	nokkur, nokkurir
sometime	nokkuru
son	son, sonar, sonur
sons	sona
speak	kveða
spirits	dísir
spoke	mælti
sprang	spratt
stayed	haldið
steadfast	staðfesti
stories	frásagnir
stormy	hvasst
strange	undarlega
stranger	undarlegri
such	slíkum
summer	sumar, sumarið
summons	kvatt
suppose	ætla
sword	sverð
swords	sverð
Syrlaekjaros (place)	sýrlækjarósi

T, t

ten	tíu
than	en, þau
that	á, að, er, sem, það, þann, þetta
that-which	er
the	að, hin, hinar, hinn, hinum, það
the-assembly	þingi, þings
the-conversion	siðaskiptið
the-days-of	dögum
the-earl	jarls
the-farmer	bóndi
the-feast	veislan
the-field	völlinn
the-home	væri
the-hopes	vonir
the-house	heim
their	sína, sinn
theirs	sinna
the-land	lands

Word List (English to Old Icelandic)

English	*Old Icelandic*	English	*Old Icelandic*
the-lands	*landa*	to-return	*snúa*
them	*þeim*	to-you	*þér*
the-matter	*mæla*	tradition	*sið*
the-men	*mönnum*	travel	*fara*
the-most	*hinn, mest*	travelled	*fór*
then	*en, þá, þann, því*	tribute	*skatt*
the-news	*tíðindi*	truely	*trúlega*
the-people	*menn*		
there	*þær, þar, þau*		
therefore	*því*		
these	*þenna*		

U, u

English	*Old Icelandic*
under	*undir*
ungladness	*ógleðjast*
union	*samlags*
until	*til*
up	*upp*
usual	*jafnan*

English	*Old Icelandic*
the-Seer	*spámaður, spámann*
the-tables	*borða*
the-town	*bæjarins*
the-women	*konurnar*
the-wood-pile	*viðköstinn*
they	*þá, þær, þau, þeim, þeir*
they-came	*komust*
they-open	*opnast*
Thidrandi (name)	*Þiðranda, Þiðrandi*
things	*hluti, hlutir, hlutum*
think	*hygg, þykir*
this	*sitt, þess, þessa, þessi, þessu, þessum, þetta*

V, v

English	*Old Icelandic*
values	*virði*

W, w

English	*Old Icelandic*
wall	*þili*
war-takings	*herfangs*
was	*er, væri, var, voru*
was-named	*hét*
was-riding	*reið*
weather	*veður*
well	*vel*
went	*gekk, gengu*
were	*er, var, voru*
what	*er, hví*
whatever	*hverigir*
when	*en, er*
where	*hvar*
whether	*hvort*
which	*en, er, sem*
while	*stundu*
white	*hvítum*
who	*er, sem*
wholly	*heilt*
whom	*sem*

English	*Old Icelandic*
this-sight	*sýnina*
Thorhall (name)	*Þórhall, Þórhalli, Þórhallur*
Thorhall's (name)	*Þórhalls*
those	*þá*
though	*þó*
thought	*hug, þótti*
three-times	*þrisvar*
Thvatta (place)	*Þvottá, Þvottár*
tidings	*tíðindi*
time	*tíma*
to	*á, að, í, til*
to-break	*boði*
to-have	*lét*
to-help	*hjálpa*
to-him	*honum*
told	*færðir, sagði*
to-me	*mér*
took	*tók*
too-late	*ofseinað*

149

Word List (English to Old Icelandic)

English	Old Icelandic
why	*hví*
widely-made-much	*viðgerðarmikið*
will	*vildi, vilja*
willed	*vildi*
window	*gluggur*
winter-night	*veturnóttum*
winters	*vetra*
wiser	*spakari*
with	*með, við*
without	*laust*
woke	*vaknaði, vöktu*
women	*konur*
words	*orð*
works	*verka*
would	*mun, mundi, mundu, munu*
would-be	*mundu*
wounded	*særðan*

Y, y

you	*þér, þig, þú, yður*
your	*yðrar*
yours	*þinn, yðrar*

A Word Comparison of Old Norse and Old Icelandic Words

A Word Comparison of Old Norse and Old Icelandic Words

Old Norse	Old Icelandic	English	Old Norse	Old Icelandic	English
áðr	áður	before	fyrr	fyrir	for
ætlat	ætlað	intended	gengit	gengið	going
aftr	aftur	back	gengr	gengur	goes
aldr	aldur	age	gera	að	that
anzar	ansar	responds	gkal	skal	shall
at	að	as	gluggr	gluggur	window
at	að	at	grimdarfulla	grimmdarfulla	cruelty-full
at	að	be	guði	guð	god
at	að	of	hafa	vilja	will
at	að	that	haft	þetta	that
at	að	the	haldit	haldið	held
at	að	to	haldit	haldið	stayed
at	gera	be	hallr	hallur	Hall (name)
atburðr	atburður	event	hefði	hefðu	have
atgervismaðr	atgervimaður	accomplished	heldr	heldur	but
austr	austur	east	hin	hinum	the
berr	ber	bears	hingat	hingað	here
bezt	best	best	hlutr	hlutur	part
blíðr	blíður	gentle	hræddr	hræddur	scared
bœjar	bæjarins	the-town	hvárt	hvort	whether
bölvuðu	bölvaðra	cursed	kallaðr	kallaður	called
borit	borið	bore	kveldit	kveldið	evening
brugðit	brugðið	broken	kvikindi	kvikvendi	creature
býðr	býður	invited	lagðr	lagður	laid
drengiliga	drengilega	bravely	lengr	lengur	longer
dyra	dura	at-the-door	lítillátr	lítillátur	modest
eðr	eða	or	lokit	lokið	ended
eðr	eða	or-that	maðr	maður	a-man
efniligastr	efnilegastur	promising	maðr	maður	man
eigi	ekki	not	makligan	maklegan	make-like
ek	eg	am-I	margr	margur	many
ek	eg	I	mikit	mikið	much
elzti	elsti	eldest	mjök	mjög	much
enn	en	and	mjúkr	mjúkur	humble
enn	en	but	morgin	morgun	morning
enn	en	than	mundri	mundu	would
enn	en	then	munit	munuð	shall
enn	en	when	munut	munuð	shall
enn	en	which	myndi	mundi	would
fœrði	færði	brought	myndi	mundu	would
fœrðir	færðir	told	nauðigr	nauðigur	compelled
frændr	frændur	kinsmen	niðr	niður	down
fróðr	fróður	a-wise	nökkurir	nokkurir	some

A Word Comparison of Old Norse and Old Icelandic Words

Old Norse	Old Icelandic	English
nökkurr	nokkur	anyone
nökkurr	nokkur	some
nökkuru	nokkuru	sometime
norrœnn	norrænn	northern
œrin	ærin	mad
œskilegra	æskilegra	desirable
of	ofseinað	too-late
ok	og	also
ok	og	and
opinberliga	opinberlega	publicly
óvinr	óvinur	enemies
riðit	riðið	riding
riðit	riðið	rode
sæti	seti	a-bench
siðaskifti	siðaskipti	conversion
siðaskifti	siðaskiptið	the-conversion
siðr	siður	a-custom
síðr	síður	less
síðu-hallr	síðu-hallur	Sidu-Hall (name)
sik	sig	himself
sjálfr	sjálfur	of-himself
sœmdar	sæmdar	honour
sonr	sonur	son
spámaðr	spámaður	a-seer
spámaðr	spámaður	the-Seer
sumarit	sumarið	summer
svá	svo	so
svarar	svaraði	answered
svarat	svarað	answered
sýrlœkjarósi	sýrlækjarósi	Syrlaekjaros (place)
þangat	þangað	from-there
þar	það	that
þat	mæla	the-matter
þat	það	it
þat	það	that
þat	það	the
þeira	þeirra	of-them
þik	þig	you
þórhallr	þórhallur	Thorhall (name)
þváttá	þvottá	Thvatta (place)
þváttár	þvottár	Thvatta (place)
þykkir	þykir	think
tjóa	það	that
unat	unað	liked
undarliga	undarlega	strange
undarligri	undarlegri	stranger
vænstr	vænstur	handsome
væra	væri	was
vánir	vonir	the-hopes
varu	voru	was
váru	voru	were
veðr	veður	weather
veizla	veisla	feast
veizlan	veislan	the-feast
veizlu	veislu	feast
verit	verið	been
vetrnóttum	veturnóttum	winter-night
viðgerðarmikit	viðgerðarmikið	widely-made-much
vilda	vildi	will
virðist	virtist	seeming
vitat	vitað	known
yðr	yður	you
yztr	ystur	outer

www.ingramcontent.com/pod-product-compliance
Lightning Source LLC
Chambersburg PA
CBHW051411070526
44584CB00023B/3379